Race-ing
Moral
Formation

Race-ing Moral Formation

African American Perspectives on Care and Justice

EDITED BY

VANESSA SIDDLE WALKER
JOHN R. SNAREY

FOREWORD BY

CAROL GILLIGAN AND JANIE WARD

Teachers College
Columbia University
New York and London

Published by Teachers College Press, 1234 Amsterdam Avenue, New York, NY 10027

The epigraph for chapter 3 are lyrics from "No Mirrors in My Nana's House." Words and music by Ysaye M. Barnwell. © 1991 by Barnwell's Notes Publishing. Used with permission.

Library of Congress Cataloging-in-Publication Data

Race-ing moral formation : African American perspectives on care and justice / edited by Vanessa Siddle Walker, John R. Snarey.
    p. cm.
    Includes bibliographical references (p.) and index.
    ISBN 0-8077-4449-2 (pbk. : alk. paper) — ISBN 0-8077-4450-6 (cloth : alk. paper)
    1. African Americans—Social conditions. 2. African Americans—Psychology. 3. African Americans—Education. 4. Social justice—United States. 5. Moral education—United States. 6. African American philosophy. 7. Ethics—United States. 8. Social values—United States. 9. United States—Race relations. 10. United States—Moral conditions. I. Siddle Walker, Vanessa. II. Snarey, John R., 1948–

E185.86.R244 2004
170'.89'96073—dc22   2003070315

ISBN 0-8077-4449-2 (paper)
ISBN 0-8077-4450-6 (cloth)

Printed on acid-free paper

Manufactured in the United States of America

11 10 09 08 07 06 05 04   8 7 6 5 4 3 2 1

for
Sarah and Elizabeth

Contents

Foreword

Carol Gilligan and Janie Ward

Carol: "What if Heinz were Black?" I remember the moment—the voice of an African American student electrifying the large lecture hall in the staid Georgian building where I was teaching a course on moral development, his question suddenly illuminating the unspoken: the presumption that Heinz was White, that if he stole an over-priced drug to save his wife's life, a judge would agree that stealing in this case was the right thing to do. The moral logic was impeccable, but what if Heinz were Black? What would the judge do then? Wouldn't the story change? Wouldn't the conversation with the judge be different? We all knew that it would.

Janie: I was a student in the class and I recall the day when Heinz's race became explicit and the room suddenly fell silent. Chalos and Ronnie Blakeney had raised this question about Heinz in the weekly seminar that met around the long oval table in Larry Kohlberg's office. They were teaching assistants in the course. The voices of African American students were changing the conversation about moral development and moral education.

Carol: It was the 1970s, the time of a sudden and startling recognition that theories of psychological development seen as objective and culturally neutral were being driven by considerations of race and gender. Psychologists were selecting all-White, all-male samples for the research on which they based their theories of human development; Kohlberg derived his six stages of moral development from a longitudinal study of 84 White boys. The tacit assumption was that you could leave out African Americans and women and miss nothing of significance.

Race and gender were associated with disadvantage, with low social class and educational limitation. The civil rights movement and the women's movement challenged these systemic injustices; psychologists and educators sought to reduce the costs of discrimination, prejudice, and trauma. But at this moment of turn in intellectual history, the blindness to race and gender revealed the power of culture to conceal the obvious. Within the field of psychology, the error was unmistakable: White men are not a representative sample of humans.

What had been lost by not listening to women? How would the voices of African Americans inform the understanding of morality and moral development? *Race-ing Moral Formation* takes up these questions, zeroing in on the intersections of justice and care in African American culture and focusing on the situation of Black women to explore the connections between race and gender. My eye is caught by the fact that Vanessa Siddle Walker and John Snarey are both parents of African American daughters.

In a Different Voice (1982) introduced an ethic of care to capture a view of the human condition that starts from a premise of connectedness rather than from an assumption of separateness. The voices of women, White and African American, who participated in the abortion-decision study, articulated a reality of relationship that called for a different way of speaking about self and about morality. In the words of Martin Luther King, writing from the Birmingham jail, "we are caught in an inescapable network of mutuality, tied in a single garment of destiny. Whatever affects one directly affects all indirectly." Acting in the human world was like walking on a trampoline.

But women's voices also called attention to a morality of selflessness, held up as the feminine ideal—the morality of the "angel in the house." Sojourner Truth had challenged this image of a White woman on a pedestal by asking, "Ain't I a woman?" Virginia Woolf shattered the image in freeing herself to write. Selflessness signified an absence of self: an abdication of voice and an evasion of responsibility and relationship. Feminism challenged this model of relationships and took on the accusation of selfishness that condemned the woman who thought and spoke for herself.

In developing an ethic of care, I sought to ground morality in a psychology of relationship and to address the dilemmas that arose in seeking to act responsively and responsibly in connection with others and with oneself. Voice was at the heart of this project, its acoustics illuminating how a person's inner world can come into the outer world and how the outer world (the voices of others) can enter the chamber of the self, like breathing out and breathing in. By starting from a premise of connectedness rather than separateness, the ethic of care shifted the paradigm of psychological theory and research, changing the way of conceiving and speaking about self and relationship, morality and development. In "The Origins of Morality in Early Childhood Relationships," Grant Wiggins and I (1987) compare this paradigm shift to a Gestalt reorganization of the field.

The papers collected in this volume reveal the vital contribution of African American voices to understanding the relationship between justice and care. They extend the work of Janie Ward, who highlighted the tradition of resistance in African American culture and drew on the wisdom of African American families to elucidate what she calls "resistance for transformation." What if Heinz and his wife were Black; what would they tell us about the intersections of race and gender and how would they transform our understanding of moral development and moral education?

Janie: Upon review of the mainstream literature in the fields of moral psychology and moral education, it wouldn't take long to conclude that very little has been said about African American moral insights, mature judgments, or uplifting traditions. The study of race and morality tends to proceed down two curious paths. In one, the investigation of racial difference finds that Blacks, when compared to their White counterparts, nearly always measure up as "less than." Following the other trail—adopting a colorblind philosophy and thus allowing race and ethnicity to fall victim to claims of universality—isn't much better. Believing little can be learned from them, few of these other researchers have explored the moral values, perspectives, and practices of African Americans. This volume is a welcome corrective to this shamefully silenced discourse.

African Americans, on the other hand, have always been thinking about and acting on moral principles. Throughout our history, from plantation proverbs to freedom songs, we have grappled with questions about who we are as an African people, and where we are headed. The moral lessons we've learned and passed on have had to be culturally specific, responsive to the effects of injustice that have circumscribed our lives, and respectful of the care, connectedness, and interdependence that assured our survival through the best and the worst of times.

Our earlier scholars, such as W. E. B. Dubois, called it "double consciousness," the need African Americans feel to hold fast to a belief, value, or sense of reality that is different from the one being promoted. Interpreting those dominant knowledge claims and, when necessary, finding the strength to challenge them has in large part been responsible for generating the strength we have needed to keep believing in our own humanity and the power to assert our moral authority in the face of continuing injustice and intolerance.

The authors in this volume provide abundant evidence of the passion for justice and long, rich traditions of care that have characterized African American individuals, families, and communities. With careful scrutiny and loving exactitude the authors have uncovered the moral treasures of a people—wisdom, the enduring power of truth, values that support and sustain individual and community development against all odds, and a trust in their own voices and perspectives. As John Snarey and Vanessa Siddle Walker have so eloquently argued, African Americans have never dichotomized justice and care into separate and exclusive domains. The ways in which these moral orientations take root and reside in the lives of African American people are beautifully illustrated within these pages. They push our thinking, test our assumptions, and give us much to consider.

This volume has been a long time coming, and we are all enriched by its arrival. The authors in these pages have shown us once and for all that race matters, in positive and constructive ways.

Acknowledgments

We welcome this opportunity to express our appreciation for the many ways in which others have helped to make this book possible.

Emory University provided an interdisciplinary environment that nurtured our collaboration, for which we are most thankful. Among our faculty colleagues, Jacqueline Jordan Irvine, Noel Erskine, Mary Elizabeth Moore, Luther Smith, Alton Pollard, Karen Scheib, and Teresa Fry Brown stand out for their supportive feedback. The book manuscript was pilot tested in our classes, and we are thankful for the valuable feedback received from our student colleagues. Student and faculty colleagues also were helpful in identifying chapter-correlated films for classroom use; these recommended films are listed in Appendix A.

We composed an external board for peer review of each manuscript under consideration, and each accepted chapter also received additional comments and suggestions from a second set of external reviewers. We wish to thank these reviewers: Mary Lou Arnold, Jane S. Attanucci, Mary F. Belenky, William Belanger, Kathy Clark, Deborah Deemer, Robert Ethridge, Kristine Hansen, Bob Howard, Jacqueline Jordan Irvine, Dierdre Kelly, Joyce King, Marion Mason-Muir, Adam Niemczynski, Nel Noddings, Clark Power, Howard B. Radest, Michelle M. Robbins, Kim Schonert-Reichl, Steve Thoma, Larry Walker, Janie Ward, and Gillian Wark.

Dedicated editorial assistance was provided by Carol Snarey, Jennifer Snyder, and Lynn Bridgers; meticulous bibliographic research assistance was provided by Emily Denmark, Elizabeth Snarey, and Anika Jones. Careful word processing assistance was provided by Sharon Ananthasane and Sandra Tucker.

Most of all, we must thank our editor, Susan Liddicoat, at Teachers College Press. Her belief in the importance of this project and her attentive and detailed feedback prompted us to craft a product that neither of us could have envisioned without her editorial guidance.

Race Matters in Moral Formation

Vanessa Siddle Walker and John R. Snarey

I remember the voices of resistance all this time. Chalos and Ronnie Blakeney asking what if Heinz were Black, what would the judge do then? Wouldn't the story change? Wouldn't the conversation with the judge be different? We all knew that it would.
—Carol Gilligan in "Remembering Larry"

THE QUESTION raised by Charles and Ronnie Blakeney around Lawrence Kohlberg and Carol Gilligan's seminar table remains as important today as it was at first asking. In fact, it prophetically forecast the new understanding of moral formation pursued in this volume.

WHERE WE SAT AT THE TABLE

The past intersected the present as we sat at the table in our favorite breakfast meeting spot. We were John and Vanessa, a White male and an African American female, who together engaged in an academic conversation about the theoretical frameworks that Lawrence Kohlberg and Carol Gilligan had established, debated, and ultimately used to change the landscape of developmental psychology. Resistant and annoyed, Vanessa finally acknowledged the exasperation that never allowed her to fully engage the models. "I don't see how these theories account for the African American experience in this country," she proclaimed. Pause. "I don't see why we have to be bound by them."

The frank discussion of "similarity" and "difference" that followed had been in the making for some time. We had both been graduate students on Appian Way at the Harvard Graduate School of Education in the same decade when the Kohlberg-Gilligan debate was at its height. We had both studied with Carol, and one of us also with Larry. Nevertheless, our graduate paths never crossed in Cambridge and, later, our intellectual interests had paved different directions, as colleagues at Emory University. As we reviewed the similarity in our pasts, our differences now also seemed understandable.

John had entered the Kohlberg-Gilligan debate as a student, embracing both Kohlberg's developmental theory and elements of Gilligan's critique. Working with Carol Gilligan and her teaching assistants, Ronnie and Chalos Blakeney, he began to explore cultural and gender differences in his course paper, "Nasreen Kahn: The Moral Development of a Pakistani Muslim Girl." When he left Harvard, John was contributing his own cross-cultural critique to the ongoing conversation.

Looking back, however, he knew that he had intuitively perceived other problems during his student years. While assisting with interviewing at the sites of Kohlberg's high school interventions, John sensed that the model of moral education was not sensitive to working-class and African American voices. He was eventually able to address the issue of social-class bias (Snarey, 1995), but he felt unqualified to speak on matters of racial difference in moral voice.

Vanessa had been intrigued by the argument for gender differences in moral reasoning when *In a Different Voice* was first published. Nevertheless, she had usually felt distanced from the discussions that took place in Carol Gilligan's class. Somehow, nothing about the debate resonated—it was almost as though she was listening in on someone else's heated argument but was untouched by its intensity. Only the moral-dilemma research paper she submitted to the teaching assistant, Janie Ward, had engaged her. It included African American teenagers' reactions to the "porcupine dilemma," a scenario in which a prickly porcupine begged his way into the home of a family of moles and then refused to leave when he was causing them discomfort. The teenagers' reactions to the dilemma were both unfavorable and different from reactions that others had found. Vanessa knew that the teenager's voices and her own voice sounded off key in a White feminist reading of the dilemma. In any case, her interests were leading her to historical scholarship (Siddle Walker, 1996).

How was it that we had responded to the same conversation so differently? Upon reflection, we realized that we had actually heard, so to speak, different conversations and constructed different areas of engagement and disengagement. Were our different constructions rooted in age, gender, social class, religion, and training differences? Or were they most significantly processed, both then and now, under the influence of our racial-ethnic identities? Once we addressed *who* we were in the story and how our experiences may have influenced the ways in which we engaged the theories, we were able to begin a genuine partnership based on the creative dissonance of difference.

"We don't have to be bound by the theories," John acknowledged as we processed our individual responses to the moral development theoretical frames. With that breakthrough, an intensely informative, almost exhilarating collaboration took shape over the years, as our voices refracted each other with, "Yeah, that makes sense" and "I never thought of it that way before" and "Write that down." Our mutual interests in African American issues of equity fueled the desire to know how an African American voice might reshape theories of moral development. John needed to know because his work on moral development led him to a commitment to pluralism and the belief that the field desperately needed a systematic portrayal of African American moral perspectives. Vanessa needed to know because her historical scholarship led her to the inescapable conclusion that care and justice were central, recurring themes in African American educational history and that African Americans could contribute in powerful ways to the shaping of moral development theory.

JOIN US AT THE TABLE

This collaboration has demanded that we go beyond our academic, gender, and ethnic differences to envision a new understanding of moral development. We now invite you to join us at the table to explore the role of race in moral formation and the contribution of African American voices to moral education. Will welcoming African American voices into the center of the moral development conversation change the nature of the way we understand justice and care formation? Although we recognize the lack of empirical data justifying the use of *race* as a term to categorize people, we also understand that "race" is what historically has been used to give privilege to one group over another. Indeed, the influence of race is so pervasive that a failure to talk about it usually means that the academic theories espoused predominately reflect the attitudes, values, and beliefs of Whites and omit, or assume compliance with, the perspectives of others. Moral-formation theory and practice have developed in this manner. What, we wondered, would happen if we raced (African Americanized) theories of moral formation?

MORAL DEVELOPMENT THEORY IN A CAPSULE

Carol Gilligan and Lawrence Kohlberg both declared repeatedly that education is fundamentally a moral endeavor (Gilligan, 1982; Gilligan, Lyons, & Hanmer, 1990; Kohlberg & Mayer, 1972; Power, Higgins & Kohlberg, 1989). They also acknowledged that both care and justice matter in moral education (Gilligan, Ward, Taylor, & Bardige, 1988; Kohlberg, 1984). Yet the field of the psychology of moral development and moral education is generally bifurcated between Kohlberg-inspired advocates of an ethic of justice and Gilligan-inspired advocates of an ethic of care.

A care orientation, according to developmental and educational psychologist Carol Gilligan (1982), reflects the presence of benevolence and compassion. A caring person treats another person with sensitive discernment of, and response to, his or her contextually embedded need. Care means liberating others from their state of need and actively promoting their welfare; care additionally means being oriented toward ethics grounded in empathy rather than in dispassionate abstract ethical principles. Elements of an ethic of care have been advocated in the works of both male and female ethicists (e.g., David Hume, 1875; Milton Mayeroff, 1971; Nel Noddings, 1984).

A justice orientation, according to developmental and educational psychologist Lawrence Kohlberg (1984), concerns fairness and impartiality. A just or fair person aims to treat another person as an end in himself or herself rather than simply as a means to an end. Justice means liberating others from injustice and orienting oneself away from biases and partial passions and toward universal ethical principles. Elements of an ethic of justice also have been advocated by both female and male ethicists (e.g., Immanuel Kant, 1797; Martha Nussbaum, 2000; John Rawls, 1971).

Indeed, the debate has confirmed a number of striking contrasts between these two ethical orientations. These include such differences as what a person recognizes to be a moral dilemma; the ethical values, virtues, or principles used to interpret a moral dilemma; the preferred methods of dilemma resolution; and the ultimate end point of moral maturity to which they point (see Figure 1). This debate, however, has largely taken place in an arena dominated by White researchers. How did this dynamic affect the field of moral develop-

FIGURE 1. The Ethical Voices of Care and Justice

An Ethic of Care	An Ethic of Justice
To recognize a moral dilemma, a person using an ethic of care tends to quickly identify situations or a dimension of a situation that involves abandonment, detachment, gender bias, hurt, pain, and violations of interpersonal intimacy.	*To recognize a moral dilemma*, a person using an ethic of justice tends to quickly see situations or elements of a situation that involve inequality, oppression, unfairness, or violations of personal autonomy.
To interpret a moral dilemma, a person using an ethic of care tends to stress the virtues of attachment, attending to, balancing a recognition of the needs of all involved with their respective communities, claiming the integrity of linkages between the generations, maintaining interpersonal connection, and valuing uniqueness (e.g., care or love for a person in all of his or her subtle distinctiveness).	*To interpret a moral dilemma*, a person using an ethic of justice tends to stress principles of contractual obligations, equal respect, equal rights, formal equality, integrity of the individual life cycle, reciprocity, and universal claims (e.g., impartial fairness or respect for all persons).
To resolve a dilemma through care, procedural emphasis is placed on attaining a sense of community consensus, conversation and mutual communication, maintaining connection, using psychological wisdom, the logic of affect, sensitivity to context, and responding to need.	*To resolve a dilemma*, a person using an ethic of justice places procedural emphasis on individual contemplation, using philosophical wisdom and the logic of reason, and attaining a clear decision regarding an impartial, right, and objective answer to the moral dilemma.
A mature person, from an ethic-of-care perspective, is committed to consensually chosen moral values and the welfare of the generations; an ideal world is characterized by nonviolence.	*A mature person*, from an ethic-of-justice perspective, is someone committed to universal ethical principles and the welfare of each individual; an ideal world is characterized by equality.

ment, particularly in the models of care and justice ethics? In an often-cited statement, Jim Banks (1993) argues, confirming the views of sociologist Robert Merton (1973) and African American educator Anna Julia Cooper (1892), that the perspectives of both "insiders" and "outsiders" are needed to "enlarge" our "view of social reality" (p. 6). Thus, the lack of an African American perspective in the conversation not only limits the spectrum of voices, but also continues to isolate the most notably missing and potentially enriching voice.

AN AFRICAN AMERICAN VOICE OF CARE-AND-JUSTICE

Pluralism and complexity are inherent in moral conversations and the moral life. We believe that placing African Americans at the center of the discussion may cause biased moral assumptions to unravel and new complexity to be woven into the fabric of care, justice, and moral education.

In terms of the overall care-versus-justice debate, historical and cultural patterns suggest that African Americans find it unnatural to subordinate either care to justice or justice to care and generally listen with suspicion when theorists sharply separate care and justice into exclusive stratospheres. When this dichotomy is applied to education, for instance, African Americans seek schools that are "just" for their children in distribution of resources, facilities, and educational opportunity. Simultaneously, however, they seek schools that provide caring environments for their children. The case of *Roberts v. City of Boston* provides an apt demonstration of this tension. In 1787, Blacks, claiming that their children were not served well or cared for in the public schools of Boston where both Black and White children could attend schools together, petitioned the school board to furnish them with schools where the needs of their children could be met. The school board finally granted segregated schools, which built upon the industry of African American parents who had begun to supply schooling for their children and provided the hope that Black children could be carefully nurtured. The parents gradually realized, however, that they were being required to sacrifice the material advantages they could have received in desegregated schools. Consequently, a few decades later, they petitioned the school board, and eventually initiated a lawsuit, demanding that they receive desegregated schools or justice in equity of resources within the school system (Schultz, 1973). At the root of their parental dilemma, and in today's manifestations of similar school desegregation cases being litigated (Siddle Walker, 1998), is the desire that African American students receive both fairness in the distribution of resources and care-fullness in the provision of nurture.

African Americans see both justice and care as necessary for their children's development. Thus, on one level, an either-or debate on the relative merits of care versus justice misses the point: African American communities generally want the justice of equality of opportunity and, simultaneously, the care that is associated with school success. But on another level, this is precisely the point: Just as feminist ethicists questioned the gender inclusiveness of an ethic of male-defined justice and advanced an ethic of care, African American parents question the racial inclusiveness of a primarily White-defined dichotomy of justice *versus* care.

Care and justice, in summary, cannot be dichotomized or simply reduced to one voice. To begin to reorient the conversation, and orient the reader in this book, we hold up the following five African American justice and care basic values. While we do not argue that these are uniquely African American values or that they encompass all African Americans, we believe that they provide a useful rubric for enlarging our understandings of care and justice and assist in providing a foundation that will help reshape the moral discussion.

1. Race Is Not Subordinate to Gender

Authors of empirical studies and theoretical essays seeking to explore and expand the boundaries of care and justice have primarily concentrated on gender differences (cf. Brabeck, 1989; Gilligan et al., 1988; Jaffee & Hyde, 2000; Puka, 1994b; Thoma, 1986; Walker, 1995). To the surprise of some, research has shown that both women and men are able to use the ethical voices of both justice and care with equal sophistication. To the surprise of others, however, women and men often have a significantly different affinity for, and actual use of, care and justice reasoning. Gendered ethical voices also have been demonstrated to vary to some degree, according to the type of moral dilemma (Wark & Krebs, 1996). Little attention, however, has been paid to how caring and fairness may be constructed, implemented, and received in ways that vary according to race. Because White men and women have primarily developed the theory and conducted the research in these fields, research on gendered voices, not surprisingly, has taken priority over research on raced voices. From the perspective of many African American women and men, however, race would be an equally viable primary focus.

Recognizing that African American interests are not well represented in gender studies, many African American feminists prefer to refer to themselves as *womanists*, a term popularized by African American writer Alice Walker and derived from "the Black folk expression of mothers to female children" who wanted "to know more and in greater depth than is considered 'good' for one" (Walker, 1983,

p. xi). Many African American male scholars share the suspicion of racial bias when White scholars prioritize ethical issues related to gender over those related to race. Although "everyone" understands that race, gender, and social class are woven into complex overlapping social categories, African Americans know from experience that—whether they are upper class and female, working class and male, or middle class and bisexual—race is foremost the most prominent feature that defines how they are categorized. In 1903, William E. B. Du Bois observed that "at the dawning of the Twentieth Century," the major problem of our nation was "the problem of the color line" (p. xi). Now, in the 21st century in the United States, the thread in the web that carries the most weight is still race.

2. Resistance Is Not Subordinate to Accommodation

In the tangle of this oppressive web, African American leaders have embraced both resistance and accommodation as fundamental strategies for change and empowerment. The debate between Booker T. Washington (1901, 1903) and W. E. B. Du Bois (1903) on the kind of curriculum to offer African American children at the turn of the century has long been invoked by historians to illustrate a split between the African American communities that espoused opposition and those that espoused accommodation. Should the race align itself against the crucible of White discrimination, or should it accommodate to it by concentrating on internal uplift and hope from within, despite the larger structural inequalities? As some historians have characterized it, the orientations themselves were contradictory and revealed an African American division in perspective regarding strategy.

The incompleteness of this analysis becomes evident, however, when one considers the ways in which the African American community embraced both leaders and reconciled their views (e.g., Aldridge, 1999). The African American community as a whole, that is, made room for both Washington and Du Bois, since they saw both accommodation and resistance as equally necessary strategies for racial uplift (Franklin, 1990). Both orientations also can be documented in other African American educational reform leaders of the era, especially Black principals of segregated schools (Rodgers, 1976). The importance of this African American oppositional/accommodating stance has been little explored by authors of moral development literature, with the exception of Janie Ward, who has helped moral educators appreciate the moral life of African American youth. Ward (2000, cf. Green, 2002) has observed that even educators who strongly support affirmative action and equal education for African American youth find it difficult to appreciate those "loud Black girls." Their resistance, while earning them the title of "troublemakers," paradoxically seats them at the table with the likes of Martin Luther King Jr. and Malcolm X. In each case, opposition and accommodation could be practical, simultaneously employed strategies used to achieve a similar agreed-upon end.

3. Religion Is Not Subordinate to Ethics

"At the cross"—to use the customary religious language of an often-sung hymn in African American churches—the logjam of justice versus mercy was broken. Historically, many African Americans have felt strongly that moral theology is central to any conversation about justice and care. African American ethical perspectives, more specifically, are deeply rooted in West African religiosity and deeply invested in Christian moral theology, both of which affirm the equality of persons before God, including the worth of the individual and God's care for all persons (Cooper-Lewter & Mitchell, 1986, p. 95). African American theological ethics have also historically made a pilgrimage toward, and claimed, liberation. Just as God delivered his people from enslavement in Egypt, he would deliver Africans in America from the bondage of slavery in that country. Even a cursory review of the leaders of slave uprisings indicates the extent to which many viewed themselves as Moses-type deliverers of their people. Nat Turner, for example, proclaimed that "the spirit that spoke to the prophets in former days" confirmed for him the impression that he was "ordained for some great purpose in the hands of the Almighty" (Barksdale & Kinnamon, 1972, p. 166). And Harriet Tubman, the legendary conductor on the Underground Railroad, was known as "Moses."

Yet the religious dimension of moral development has been avoided by most mainstream scholars because of their "faith" that God is "nothing but" a social construction (for exceptions, see cf. Gorsuch, 1988; Kohlberg & Power, 1981; Noddings, 1993). In the historical African American religious tradition, however, grounding ethical ideals in a transcendent reality is equally a matter of faith. For most African Americans, religion supports, but is not subordinate to, ethics. Thus, contrasting religion with ethics creates a useless dichotomy. Moreover, any effort to understand the moral dimension of African American life will be diminished without an understanding of the historically central role of religion in African American views of care and justice.

4. Agency Is Not Subordinate to Legacy

A fourth basic value advanced in this book is that agency is not subordinate to the legacy of oppression. Although the oppression of African Americans is evident across time in the dehumanization embodied in the institution of slavery, the domestic terrorism of Jim Crow, and the denial of educational and job opportunities, this legacy has not created paralysis within the African American community. Rather than being overwhelmed by the continuing waves of oppression, African Americans have systematically, cooperatively, and continuously engaged in activities to define their place as Americans and create opportunities for themselves and their children. These activities continue into the present.

In contemporary settings, the struggle for agency and empowerment among African American children and youth involves an understanding of the self as agent (Curtis, 1993; Curtis-Tweed, 2003). Agency functions as an organizing construct that undergirds moral development. Agency is the individual's ability to process and structure his or her life experiences. These activities may include internal processes such as interpretation, evaluation, prioritization, self-reflection, and decision making regarding life experiences and context (Taylor, 1985).

Because American society devalues people of color, African Americans have formed a sense of agency that relies upon their self-perceptions, rather than the images depicted by the dominant culture. The elements of agency—self-reflection, consistency, personal responsibility, pride, decision-making ability, self-reliance—are characteristics that allow African American children, youth, and adults to rise above and succeed in adverse conditions (Curtis-Tweed, 2003; Taylor, 1985). The external manifestation of the results of these processes is agentic behavior (cf. Turiel, 1994). Agentic behavior may embody both socially acceptable and unacceptable behavior but, regardless of how conventional or unconventional, through such moral agency the African American community survives its legacy of oppression.

5. The Community Is Not Subordinate to the Individual

Finally, a moral legacy of the West African heritage of most African Americans is the view that action promoting the African American community's ability to survive and thrive is more mature than action that only advances an individual African American. Yet even this manner of fashioning tension between two supposedly contradictory impulses is very Anglo-American. More precisely, those who follow

African American ethics refuse to starkly dichotomize self and community. To care for the self is to care for the group, and to care for the group is to care for the self.

Although European models of care tend to emphasize caring for the individual child for whom the adult has a responsibility, African American models of care demonstrated concern for the whole group and each child (cf. Collins, 2003; Noddings, 2002; Siddle Walker, 1996; Slaughter-Defoe, 1991). While affirming the worth of the individual, an African American psychology intimates that a person is a finite being, embedded in a web of social relations and institutional structures. This web buffers both the individual and the community from the suffering created by, for instance, a shifting economy. Within communities, these ethical essentials are illustrated by the folk-cultural term *othermothering*, which refers to the ability of African American grandmothers and othermothers to assume a parental role for children with whom they may share no household bond (Fry Brown, 2000). This other-parenting was evident in interactions between African American teachers, principals, and students in many of the segregated schools in the South. African American parents and educators historically worked collectively for the good of all the children. In advancing the race, their children too would benefit. To push forward one's own child, while ignoring the needs of other children, would have been violating a cultural norm. In summary, the delineation of self-care and community care into isolated categories fashions a false dichotomy.

RACE MATTERS

Each of the preceding examples of African American values suggests that contemporary educational models of moral voices and practices of moral formation call for transformation through inclusion of African American voices. Although most "mainstream" ethical perspectives perceive these contrasting voices as sources of dissonance to be eliminated, categorized, or, at best, anxiously juggled, most African American ethical perspectives embrace their mysterious unity. By articulating these differences, we hope to refocus the moral conversation. We do not argue that the experiences described are unique to African Americans, but we do believe that a focus on African American moral values and moral education practices will create a path for the inclusion of a wider spectrum of experiences. We hope that a closer examination of other groups as well will be stimulated by this systematic explanation of one multifaceted culture.

It is important to emphasize this multifaceted nature. Anglo
Americans sometimes assume that the African American community
is, well, simply "black." There is a tendency to miss the myriad ways
in which the community is rich and varied in its social expressions.
To reflect on just one example, consider the question, What is the
Black church? Building on its roots in West African indigenous traditions, the answer today includes a heterogeneous variety of religious
social entities that range from storefront to tall-steeple churches, from
Methodist chapels to Islamic mosques, from Baptist conventions to
Catholic and Rastafarian congregations. This same diversity can be seen
through out other Black institutions. Nevertheless, woven through all
of the diverse fabrics of African American culture, are a number of
common ethical threads.

But, again, whether the ethical threads are singularly African
American or whether an African American value system shares overlapping understandings with other ethnic groups, what is significant
for this discussion is comprehending that the dominant models of justice and care ethics in the field of moral development and moral education were generated and operationalized in the context of a generally
European American psychology, philosophy, and pedagogy. These theorists implicitly assumed, of course, that their narrowly constructed
ways of listening to the world represented the full spectrum of moral
meaning. Such deafness to the voices of so many inevitably dimin-
ishes the experiences and minimizes the voices of other cultural communities. Thus, not surprisingly, Lawrence Kohlberg's definition of
justice misses or misunderstands key elements of an African American call to and proclamation of justice. Nor is it surprising that Carol
Gilligan's definition of care misses or misunderstands important aspects of an African American voice of care. This is not to say, of course,
that the theorists' models have no relevance for other racial or ethnic
cultural groups. Rather, our intent in this volume is to broaden the
conversation by including the voices of African Americans and, by affirming their centrality and relevance to the debate, expand the commonly accepted constructions of justice and care. An African American
ethic of care-and-justice does not identify with the subordination of race
to gender, resistance to accommodation, religion to ethics, agency to
legacy, or community to the individual. This unity represents the potential inherent in the African American contribution. More broadly,
the refusal to be limited by the dominant conventions thrives with the
potential of modeling a way by which other groups also can resist col-
lapsing multifaceted perspectives into a one-sided understanding and,
thereby, maintain a creative tension.

The Book's Organization and Purpose

This volume is divided and unified by two foci—moral psychology and moral education. In part 1, three chapters provide a psychological perspective on moral formation among African Americans during childhood, adolescence, and adulthood. These chapters focus on what African American voices have to teach us about moral development. In part 2, three additional chapters provide more practical, pedagogical perspectives, drawn from the past, present, and ongoing challenges of African American educational practices. These chapters focus on what African American voices have to say about promoting care, justice, and moral formation within schools. Through ideas expressed in these six chapters, we initiate a conversation on caring and justice moderated by African American values.

In our concluding chapter, we develop the five primary dual values launched in our introductory chapter and also unveil their correlated resulting virtues. These "big five" values and virtues form the developmental matrix of African American ethics. In appendix A, we provide a list of chapter-correlated films that illustrate these values, and in appendix B, we summarize the ways in which each chapter contributes to our understanding of each of the five justice-and-care primary dual values.

"We are speaking," of course, "*not* from a disinterested perspective" (Dei, 1994, p. 3). Our concerns with moral psychology, moral education, and African American ethical voices are not solely academic or professional. We both are also the parents of African American daughters. As our daughters, Sarah and Elizabeth, have grown and matured, we have worried and will continue to worry about the messages that they and all African American students are sent about their current abilities, their future possibilities, and their ultimate worth. Because care and fairness are often negligible in the experience of African American students in many school systems, even economically privileged African American students attending the so-called best schools remain very much at risk for lower performance than their White peers. That is, the care that educational institutions normally provide their students often fails to make it over the hurdles of cultural differences and racism, never really reaching many African American students.

We initiate a conversation on race and the ethics of care and justice in education because we believe that the deliberations can help educators shape some of the keys needed to unlock the development and success potential of African American children. Our intent is to heighten awareness that race does matter, and should matter positively and constructively, in understanding moral formation and supporting it through moral education.

Making Our Table Conversation Public

The conversation on the relationship between the contemporary African American values and the scholarship on care and justice is long overdue. African Americans must continue to grapple with the fact that they, collectively, face greater obstacles than their White counterparts, as indicated by a host of indicators (e.g., lower annual incomes, more health problems, lower test scores, fewer well-trained teachers, poorer schools) (Nettles & Perna, 1997, 2000). The failure to include principles of care and justice in conversations about the success of African Americans in this country may also be a failure to include a variable central to the explanation of problems encountered by the African American community. Thus, the failure to include African American perspectives in theory and research on moral formation leads to a failure to include a voice central to developing a more useful, pluralistic psychology of morality and education. We believe that the psychology of moral development and education may have an important contribution to make in and with the African American community and that the African American experience has an equally important contribution to make to our understanding of moral formation and education. We have a moral responsibility to not sit silently at the table when so much remains to be said.

PART I

AFRICAN AMERICAN PATTERNS OF MORAL FORMATION ACROSS THE LIFE SPAN

OUR MORAL psychology—the way we formulate and resolve ethical dilemmas—is a fundamental dimension of being human that evolves over the course of a person's childhood, adolescence, and adulthood. Gilligan's model of care levels (Figure 2) and Kohlberg's model of justice stages (Figure 3) both illustrate the potential evolution of a moral voice toward greater complexity and adequacy. Yet, so to speak, both models also lack color.

MORAL PSYCHOLOGY AND RACE

Lawrence Kohlberg (1970, 1975) often quoted Martin Luther King Jr.'s (1963b) "Letter From Birmingham Jail" and included King's (1967c) published version as a "required" reading in his seminar on moral and political choice to illustrate Stage 6 moral reasoning. He also regularly distributed, as a course handout, copies of *Ebony* magazine's reprint of King's "I Have a Dream" speech (1963a). Citing King along with Socrates, Abraham Lincoln, and Mahatma Gandhi in his roll call of public moral educators who paid for their dedication to justice with their lives, Kohlberg (1968a) declared:

> Martin Luther King joins a long list of people who had the arrogance not only to teach justice but to live it in such a way that other people felt uncomfortable about their own goodness, their own injustice. I have frequently heard the question, "Why King, not Carmichael or Brown?" It is not people who preach power and hate who get assassinated. They are not a threat; they are like the worst in

FIGURE 2. The Ethic of Care: Three Developmental Levels

Level 1: Caring for Self (Ethic of Survival)

The first level is characterized by caring for self in order to ensure survival. The person's concern does not distinguish what *should* be done from what she or he *wants* to do. The person basically aims to protect the self, to ensure her or his own happiness, and to avoid being hurt. The person shows little evidence of caring for other people's needs or feelings, and no consideration of abstract ethical values. The person basically sees and evaluates situations from the self's point of view and does not experience much conflict about what is right or wrong. This question only emerges if the person's own needs are in conflict, in which case she or he would have to decide which needs should come first. Generally, self-interest serves as the basis for judgment.

Level 1.5: Transition from Survival to Conventional Responsibility and Goodness

At this transition, the most important issue is the person's ability to attach or connect to others. The person first begins to understand the concepts of "selfishness" and "responsibility" and can now criticize her or his own judgment and behavior as selfish or unrealistic. This self-criticism signals a new understanding of the connection between self and others, which leads to a shift from selfishness to responsibility. The person at Level 1.5 struggles more with a moral dilemma, compared to a person at Level 1, and will not be quite as sure of what to do because she or he now has some concern for the needs of others. Nevertheless, survival of the self is still the main aim.

Level 2: Caring for Others (Ethic of Conventional Goodness)

This perspective is characterized by a strong emphasis on responsibility, commitment, and a parentlike morality that seeks to provide care for the dependent and unequal. That which is to be most avoided is hurting others, and the highest form of goodness is self-sacrificing care for others. The person adopts societal values, expresses conventionally defined goodness, and is highly dependent upon the acceptance of others. The responsibility for defining the right thing to do, in fact, rests with others (e.g., parents, the church, or society). The person will set aside her or his own needs and well-being in order to give priority to caring for others, avoiding harm, and avoiding interpersonal conflict. The person at Level 2 feels responsible for the actions of others, whereas others are responsible for the choices she or he makes. The strengths of a person in this position lie in her or his capacity for caring; however, the limitation lies in the person's felt prohibition of self-assertion. Conflict arises specifically over the issue of hurting; the person helps or protects others, often at the expense of self-harm, and avoids taking responsibility for choices made.

FIGURE 2. (continued)

Level 2.5: Transition from Conventional Goodness to Reflective Care

The transition that follows Level 2 is marked by a shift from a morality of "self-sacrifice and goodness" to "truth and honesty," as the person begins to question the morality of protecting and caring for others at her or his own expense. This leads to a somewhat confused reconsideration of the morality of self-concern and the immorality of self-sacrifice. Self-concern, that is, reappears as the person begins to ask whether it is selfish or responsible, moral or immoral, to include one's own needs and care of one's own self within the moral sphere, and still be a caring person. The person reexamines what it means to be responsible, balancing concern over what other people think against a new inner concern with the self. This new sense of responsibility places an emphasis on personal honesty. A person at the Level 2.5 transition is similar in many ways to a person at the Level 1.5 transition (e.g., both consider the needs of others, while choosing to take care of self primarily). However, a person at Level 2.5 will typically see a need to become "more selfish," whereas a person at Level 1.5 sees a need to become "less selfish."

Level 3: Caring for Both Self and Other (Ethic of Care)

The criteria for judgment are now truth and honesty. The morality of an action is judged not on the basis of how it appears to others, but by its actual intention and practical effects. A person with this perspective emphasizes the dynamics of relationships and achieves a balance between selfishness and selflessness through a new understanding of the complexity of connections between others and the self. The person is able both to see a moral situation from the perspectives of each of the others involved and to still make his or her own choices. She or he accepts responsibility for decisions and takes control of her or his life. Ethical criteria for goodness are now internal. The person balances care of self with care of others, and both are included in the purview of care. Compared to the case in Level 2.5, she or he is no longer confused or in conflict about selfishness and responsibility. Hence, the person is able to take care of herself or himself, maintain commitments to others, and minimize hurt to both the self and others.

Adapted from Gilligan (1982) and Skoe (1991, 1993).

others. It is the people who are too good for other people to take, who question the basis on which people erect their paltry sense of goodness, who die (p. 66).

Trying to make sense of King's then recent assassination, Kohlberg focused on King's call for justice, which he believed "was the essence of King's moral leadership" and the essence of his threat to the status quo (p. 69).

FIGURE 3. The Ethic of Justice: Six Developmental Stages

___

Stage 1: Obedience and Punishment Orientation

At Stage 1, what is moral is to avoid breaking rules or to comply for obedience's sake, and to avoid doing physical damage to people or property. Moral judgments are self-evident, requiring little or no justification beyond labeling. A person at Stage 1 does not realize that the interests of others may differ from his or her own. Justice is understood as strict, literal equality, with special needs or mitigating circumstances not understood or taken into consideration. In situations where an authority is involved, justice is defined as respectful obedience to the authority. The justification for moral action or doing what is right includes avoidance of penalties and the superior power of authorities.

Stage 2: Instrumental Purpose and Exchange

What is moral for the person at Stage 2 is to follow the rules when it is in the person's immediate interest to do so, especially in terms of an equal exchange, a good deal. The person now recognizes that other persons may have other interests. Justice involves relating conflicting individual interests through an instrumental exchange of services or marketplace economy: You scratch my back and I'll scratch yours. The justification for being moral is to serve one's own needs in a world where one must recognize that other people also have their own interests, which may conflict with one's own.

Stage 3: Mutual Interpersonal Expectations, Good Relations

A person at Stage 3 is able to coordinate the separate perspectives of individuals into a third-person perspective, which enables interpersonal trust, mutual relationships, loyalty, and shared moral values. What is moral is conforming to what is expected by people close to you or what people generally expect of people in one's role as son, sister, parent, and so on. Justice now can take into consideration a person's worthiness, goodness, and circumstances. The justifications for acting morally focus on the desire to be seen as a good person in one's own eyes and those of others. One should be caring of others because, if you put yourself in the other person's shoes, you would want good behavior from others.

___

One could argue, however, that King only became an intolerable threat when he demonstrated that opposition is not subordinate to accommodation. During the last year or so of his life King concluded that it was "time to break silence" and speak out more broadly against the sickness of poverty

FIGURE 3. (continued)

Stage 4: Social System and Conscience Maintenance

The right thing to do is to be a good citizen, uphold the social order, and maintain the society. What is moral involves fulfilling one's duties. Laws are to be upheld, except in extreme cases in which they conflict with other fixed social duties. Justice centers on the notions of impartiality in application of the law; procedural justice first emerges as a central concern at Stage 4. A just decision also should take into consideration a person's social merit and contribution to society. This is a social-maintenance rather than an interpersonal-maintenance perspective; being moral involves contributing to one's own society, group, or institution. The justifications for being moral are to keep the institution functioning, to maintain self-respect for having met one's defined obligations, and to avoid setting a socially disruptive precedent.

Stage 5: Prior Rights and Social Contract

What is moral is being aware that many values and rules are relative to one's group and subsuming these culturally relative values under fundamental human rights, such as the rights of life and liberty, that are logically prior to society. Such nonrelative rights are inviolable and should be built into and upheld by any society. Justice, that is, focuses on human rights or social welfare; due process is also a concern. This is a society-creating rather than a society-maintaining point of view. A social system is understood, ideally, as a social contract freely entered into. Persons at Stage 5 justify upholding the social contract because it preserves one's own rights and the rights of others, ensures impartiality, and promotes the greatest good for the greatest number.

Stage 6: Universal Ethical Principles

Deciding what is moral is guided by universal ethical principles that generate decisions by which human dignity is ensured and persons are treated as ends in themselves rather than simply as means. Particular laws or social agreements are usually valid because they rest on such ethical principles. When laws violate these principles, however, one acts in accordance with the principle. Going beyond the importance of a social contract, Stage 6 also focuses on the process by which a social agreement is reached. This is a moral-justice point of view, involving the deliberate use of justice principles, which centers on the equality of human rights and respect for the dignity of all human beings as free and equal autonomous persons. The justification for being moral is the belief, as that of a rational person, in the validity of universal moral principles that all humanity should follow and because one has made a self-conscious commitment to them.

Adapted from Kohlberg (1984), Colby and Kohlberg (1987).

in the United States and against young Black men dying in Vietnam (1967a, 1967b). He also demonstrated his increasing appreciation of some aspects of the militant Black power movement (1967c). Kohlberg was aware of this and included King's (1967a) "Declaration of Independence from the War in Vietnam" in his seminar's "recommended" reading list (Kohlberg, 1970). Still, this writing never rose above the status of a recommended reading. Neither was it cited in his publications. Finally, it was altogether ignored in later versions of Kohlberg's syllabus (Kohlberg, 1975).

Perhaps Kohlberg never quite knew how to make sense of or acknowledge this more oppositional King, whose apparently newly matured voice legitimized the need for Black people to sacrifice themselves less and to care for themselves more (hooks, 1984, 2000). But, then again, both care and justice were always present in King's ethic. According to King scholar and theological ethicist Noel Erskine (1994), for instance, a central question for King was simply, "Does God care?" As Erskine explains,

> This was the bottom line for King because it has always been the critical issue for the Black church. In a culture and community in which the assault of slavery tore many families asunder, it was important to affirm that "God is the mother to the motherless, and father to the fatherless." For these families, the church became home and God was the head of the family. For a people who were cut off from their historical and cultural roots, God was their father and mother. This caring personality could be relied upon to protect and provide. (pp. 46–47)

Martin Luther King Jr. was, in essence, a drum major for both justice and care. But more than this, King also relied upon a spiritual dimension of commitment to a people and to a cause that exceeded either definition of care or justice. King, then, like many of the concepts put forth in these chapters, could not be dichotomized into current narrow formulations of care or justice.

How might a complex voice like King's be freshly encountered in the study of developmental processes that are integral to the formation of human beings? The contributors to part 1 of this book race moral psychology by decentering it from Whiteness and opening new doors in order to learn from other racial-ethnic communities and other ethical voices. The failure to do so thus far has, in effect, led to the silence and invisibility of the African American community in the conversation.

Racial-ethnic differences in psychological functioning are largely a function of cultural, rather than biological, differences. Nevertheless, the implications of racial-ethnic differences are as far reaching as those embodied in gender differences, which are also substantially grounded in culture. Within the psychology of moral development, however, both justice- and care-oriented scholars typically assume that, aside from skin color, African American children and Anglo-American children are identical, and that psychological processes are universal (cf. Parke, 2000). "In other words," as developmental psychologist Amos Wilson (1978) states, "the Black child is a White child who 'happens' to be painted Black." Thus it is not surprising, Wilson continues, that patterns of development that characterize White middle-class children were held up as "the optimal standard" by which Black children were to be judged (p. 6).

The authors of the chapters in part 1 aim to *race moral psychology*. Involved in the race-ing of moral psychology is the willingness to reconstruct the center of the field. It means to open up a new doorway to the field that partly hinges on an African American voice.

OVERVIEW OF PART ONE: FROM A DIFFERENT COLOR TO A DIFFERENT ROOM

The authors in part 1 collectively discuss African American perspectives on the following areas: (1) care, culture, and race, with reference to the experiences of *children*; (2) moral experiences of Black *adolescents*; and (3) African American feminist ethics of *womanism*. A synopsis of each chapter follows.

In chapter 1, Audrey Thompson draws on the work of African American feminists and educational theorists and other African American scholars, to unveil the unacknowledged racism that underlies "colorblindness" as the "ideal" expression of care and justice. Utilizing examples of the difference in the childhood experiences of Black and White children, Thompson demonstrates that it is still necessary to be color conscious to recognize the extent to which skin color influences the life chances of African Americans. She argues that colorblindness functions to maintain the privileges of the privileged through a misunderstanding of racial justice and harmony that implies that race does not matter. This approach, Thompson demonstrates, is *both* uncaring (e.g., because it suppresses identities) and unjust (e.g., because it maintains social inequalities).

Central to understanding self-agency is an analysis of voice, the way the self is articulated to others. In chapter 2, Garrett Duncan analyzes the moral voices of African American adolescents. Drawing from in-depth interviews with Black teenagers and autobiographical narratives culled from Black literature, and using the concept of "double consciousness" as an interpretive framework, Duncan identifies basic conjunctive values that mediate the daily ethical experiences of contemporary Black adolescents. He posits that Black adolescents, as part of a larger African American culture, bring diasporan African and ethnic American ethical voices to bear on their experiences. He suggests that the shared knowledge base that links Black people across generations is substantially ethical in nature and that, without being aware of these basic values on some level, one cannot genuinely hear their moral voice. He also demonstrates how the study of Black culture and life can enrich our understanding of morality.

Andrea Green similarly addresses the concept of different voices in the chapter 3. Metaphorically, the "different room" reflects a separation from "positivist" truth assumptions that she sees underlying *In a Different Voice*. Green urges that the adult voices of African American women be heard on their own terms. Green captures this traditional wisdom by going beyond the "double jeopardy" approach to being "African" and "female" in America by listening to their deep "womanist" voices, which echo and extract basic ethical values and core themes from their roots in Africa and their history in America. Green suggests that womanist thought both encompasses and moderates care-and-justice ethics.

Together, these three chapters reinforce the conclusion that moral development theory cannot survive across cultural boundaries until it manifests the pluralism necessary to allow the work to honor diversity. Furthermore, they reclaim the African American voice as central to the theory's ability to thrive.

CHAPTER 1

Caring and Colortalk: Childhood Innocence in White and Black

Audrey Thompson

> Anyone can fly. All you need is somewhere to go that you can't get to any other way.
>
> —Faith Ringgold, *Tar Beach*

TAR BEACH, by African American artist and feminist Faith Ring-gold (1991), is a children's story about the remembered joy of childhood summer nights on a city rooftop, with family and friends gathering to enjoy food, company, the breeze, and the view. Geographically specific, *Tar Beach* conveys Ringgold's love of New York, of the George Washington Bridge, and of the rooftop—the "tar beach" of the title—where Cassie, a young African American–American Indian girl, can revel in the beauty of her world. So magical, so powerful is Cassie's sense of that world that she feels as if she can fly high above the city. It is her world, and if she wants, she can wear the lights on the bridge like a necklace. Lyrically, *Tar Beach* captures a child's-eye view of the world. But for all its joyousness, it is not the conventional Western childhood story about a time of innocence—the time before the grimmer realities of the world make themselves known. While *Tar Beach* is far from bleak, it does not hide from the knowledge of oppression.

Cassie is under no illusions as to the poverty that worries her mother and the racism that prevents her father from finding work. Indeed, her dream of flying over the bridge is one with her dream of flying to freedom—of saving her family from racism and poverty. Told from Cassie's sky-high vantage point, the story thrills at childhood's secrecy and power and imagines using that power to change the world. The grown-ups fail to notice Cassie soaring high above their heads; only her little brother sees her. Free of supervision, Cassie flies over the city, claiming ownership of the local union headquarters so that her father can become a member and find work, and so that the family "can have ice cream every night for dessert" (p.18). Just to make sure, she flies over the ice cream factory and claims that too.

A story about childhood pleasures like ice cream as well as supposedly adult concerns such as poverty, *Tar Beach* intertwines the knowledge of racism and struggle with a magical sense of the world and its possibilities. Like African American poet Nikki Giovanni (1980), who hopes that no White person writes about her, because "they'll probably talk about my hard childhood and never understand that all the while I was quite happy" (p. 16), Ringgold celebrates the happiness of an African American childhood. At the same time, though, she shows us the historical, economic, racial, and political realities against which the child dreams her dream of freedom. It is a narrative strikingly different from that which Whites usually tell about children and race.

White culture has constructed childhood as colorblind almost by definition. It is as if the lives of children were so distinct from the lives of adults, so much a separate estate, that any social markers that the dominant culture recognizes among adults are irrelevant to children. Yet in treating childhood as a universal state in which race and other social distinctions do not matter, we celebrate and protect a sentimental conception of childhood as apolitical while preserving the political status quo into which children will eventually be inducted. Treating childhood as colorblind is by no means incompatible with racism.

In the segregationist South, for example, Black and White children were allowed to play together until they reached school age, since "in the white southern mind small black children were not a bad influence on small white children" (Haskins, 1986, p. 89). Until the age of about 7, therefore, Martin Luther King Jr. and his young White "friend had played together, ridden their bicycles together, and been welcome into each other's homes." One day, however, "his best friend's mother informed him in a hesitant voice that perhaps he should not come around anymore" (p. 89). In a racist society, Black children cannot be protected indefinitely from the knowledge of racism. Yet White children, because they are not on the receiving end of racism, may remain more or less blind to it.

Just as *Tar Beach* speaks to the knowledge that a Black child may have of racism, the picture book *Dear Willie Rudd*, by Libba Moore Gray (1993), testifies to the racial obliviousness common among White children. The story concerns "Miss Elizabeth," a southern White woman in her 50s, who, in reflecting back upon her childhood, realizes how she took for granted the Black woman who had washed her family's floors, prepared their meals, and watched over her. Only now, half a century later, does Miss Elizabeth begin to view the Black woman, Willie Rudd, as an equal. In her imagination, she invites Mrs. Rudd in at the front door, rather than having her come round to the back; they sit next to each other at the front of the bus, and they eat together at the same table. Yet even in Miss Elizabeth's mature understanding, these gestures at equality do not extend beyond inclusion (meaning that Willie Rudd once again is the young Elizabeth's companion, but this time on equal terms). For Miss Elizabeth, rethinking their relationship on more equal terms does not mean interrogating the racialized class relations that kept Mrs. Rudd on her knees, scrubbing a White family's floors, or confronting the racial privilege that allowed a little White girl to be waited on, sung to, and cared for by a Black maid.

As framed by the author, Miss Elizabeth's bittersweet memories form a poignant tale of love and regret, rather than a story of oppression. Betraying an understanding of racial hierarchies as uncritical as that of her protagonist, Gray refers to the White woman as Miss Elizabeth but never problematizes Miss Elizabeth's remembrance of Mrs. Rudd as Willie. Even when the authorial voice shifts away from the child's-eye view, Mrs. Rudd is identified as Willie Rudd, in keeping with the racist White southern convention of denying African Americans the courtesy titles Mr., Mrs., or Miss as terms of respect. The book's child-centered perspective thus reinscribes the very racism that the author means to challenge. By failing to question either the etiquette of racism whereby a White child may call a Black adult by her first name or the sense of intimacy and entitlement that prevents Miss Elizabeth from addressing her apology to "Dear Mrs. Rudd," instead of "Dear Willie Rudd," the author sentimentalizes the liberties that Whites take with African Americans.

The author's lack of racial awareness is perhaps also reflected in her character's vagueness about the nature of the racist offenses her family committed. Even 50 years later, Miss Elizabeth's sense of her family's racist treatment of Willie Rudd remains indefinite enough that she can say to her only, "I'm sorry for anything any of us might have done to make you sad" (p. 12). It is unclear whether Miss Elizabeth's awareness of what counts as racism is actually this ill formed or whether, instead, her vagueness stands in for the kind of racial understanding that Gray considers appropriate to her child-readers. Perhaps both are the case. Given the training in colorblindness that White children receive, it should not be surprising that Miss Elizabeth took some 50 years to begin to feel troubled in her mind about her family's racism. As a child she had never thought about the implications of having a Black maid, because she didn't need to think about the maid at all: It was her privilege to be ignorant.

Contrary to mainstream White beliefs about childhood and innocence, however, such racial obliviousness is not an automatic attribute of childhood. It is acquired as a result of both social privilege and education in colorblind racial etiquette. Most U.S. schools and teacher education programs, for example, avoid the topics of race and racism (Chalmers, 1997; Kailin, 1999; Kelly, 1998; Kohl, 1995). This willed colorblindness assumes that the essence of racism lies in *noticing* difference, since, in a racist society, colors other than that associated with the dominant group are stigmatized. Teachers who announce, "In this class, we're all purple polka-dotted!" are concerned with reassuring their non-White students that no one notices their color. Inevitably, however, this euphemistic colortalk alerts students that color *matters*, but that it is considered polite to act as if one did not notice. This politeness makes no sense unless being of different colors is somehow shameful (Thompson, 1999). Colorblindness is parasitic on racism: It is only in a racist society that pretending not to notice color could be construed as a virtuous act. If child-centered educators are to address Black, Brown, and White students' actual situations, histories, cultures, and daily struggles, they cannot suppress colortalk.

Acknowledging racial identity, culture, racism, and racial privilege as factors that shape and color experience, colortalk recognizes that a person's color is a significant dimension of her or his experience. Because theories of caring in education address the nurturing practices and values that organize much of child-centered teaching, they are potentially a key forum in which to challenge the colorblindness of much of child-centered education. For the most part, however, educational theories of care themselves have been colorblind (e.g., Brown & Gilligan, 1992; Martin, 1992; Noddings, 1992). Even when such theories explicitly seek to address the needs of children and adolescents of all races (e.g., Martin, 1992; Taylor, Gilligan, & Sullivan, 1995), they remain effectively colorblind because they do not examine the Whiteness of their underlying assumptions and commitments.

WHITE THEORIES OF CARE

The central purpose of most White theories of care has been to offer a corrective to the universalism claimed for theories of justice. Building on Gilligan's, Noddings's, and other caring theorists' analyses, scholars researching the ethics of care have focused on the nurturing practices commonly regarded as women's work. The ethical ideal to which women and girls appeal, these theorists argue, is referenced not to abstract, disinterested principles of justice, but to the lived experience of caring. Often, caring is associated with the "ideal" home or with "authentic," intimate relationships.

From the perspective of Black feminism, however, the moral ideal set forth in much of the mainstream ethics of care literature may be as problematic in its own way as the justice ideal it is meant to challenge. Most of the mainstream literature on caring has assumed that White, middle-class, heterosexual conceptions of caring were (or ought to be) universal. Even when applying their work to students of color, White researchers have tended to look for the culturally White practices and values that they—and their theories—already recognize as caring. Yet not only is the mainstream ideal of caring by no means universal, but its very status *as* an ideal is problematic. Many, if not most, women of color have to cope with "real-lived" conditions that bear little resemblance to the choice-laden circumstances posited for the moral individual (Cannon, 1988, pp. 2–5). Indeed, the assumption that the practice of maternal caring is connected to an ideal domestic environment is likely to add yet another form of pressure to the lives of women already overburdened with cares, so that a Black woman who works outside the home as her family's primary breadwinner, for example, may be castigated both for failing to uphold standards of domestic order and for failing to give her children and husband sufficient attention (Tice, 1998).

Ethical formulas that assume White-on-White and White-on-Black ideals also eclipse the richness of Black-on-Black moral relationships. The sentimental language of love so familiar to White, middle-class mothers, for instance, may fail to capture the experience of many African American families. Looking back on her childhood, Faith Ringgold (1995) recalls, "When I was growing up, I never heard anyone mention giving children love." Love was never talked about. But the reality of love was unmistakable.

> We got attention, care, a comfortable and good home, clothes and food, and all of Mother's time and energy. What more could "love" bring? My

mother gave us the kind of love that was lived, rather than verbalized. She never actually said the words "I love you," but we all knew she did. (p. 7)

Because Ringgold and her sister and brother did not reference mother love to an ideal of verbalized affection, they knew they were loved. Those who expect love to look like the White, middle-class ideal, however, may fail to recognize particular African American approaches to caring, since the White, middle-class—often sentimental—ideal of mother love does not address the caring work of women who put their life's energy into striving to create a better future for their children.

In the remainder of this discussion, I revisit four of the moral themes that emerged from *In a Different Voice* (Gilligan, 1982):

1. The centrality of authentic, trustworthy relationships
2. The salience of the standpoint from which virtues and vices are identified
3. The adoption of a pragmatic orientation toward survival
4. The issue of exploitative and oppressive social relations

As theorized by Cannon (1988), Collins (1990), Ward (1990, 1995), hooks (1984), Eugene (1989), James (1993), and Walker (1983), these themes take on an importantly different significance from that given to them in most White versions of the ethics of care.

BLACK FEMINIST ETHICS

Both for cultural reasons and because Black resistance to oppression requires the support of a collective, expectations of caring in Black communities are not confined to the individual, private-sphere practices recognized in White theories of caring or justice. In Kohlberg's (1981) work, respondents' notions of justice are categorized in terms of their analyses of hypothetical moral scenarios. For example, respondents to the famous Heinz dilemma are asked whether Heinz should steal a life-saving drug or let his wife die for lack of the drug. Girls and women, Gilligan (1982) found, often objected both to the implausible either-or framing of the narrative and to the implication that the druggist—who had refused to accept anything less than the full market value for the drug—was somehow an innocent bystander.

Faced with this same scenario, many African American respondents might object that, had Heinz been a member of an African American community, he would not have assumed that his only options for obtaining the medicine were either to buy it himself or to steal it. A longstanding ethic in African American communities is reliance on and commitment to both family and communal networks of support (Eugene, 1989; James, 1993). In the slaveholding South, for example, it was usually financially impossible for free Black individuals to purchase family members' freedom on their own, and Blacks "at once depended upon and supported their kin and communal networks as they struggled to secure their freedom" (Corrigan, 1994, p. 165). An African American in Heinz's place normally would have looked to friends, family, the community, and the Black Church for help. Such a response to the Heinz dilemma would resemble the pattern in White girls' and women's responses, yet also would be importantly different in emphasizing cultural, communal, and political solidarity in addition to interpersonal networks. A Black ethic of care emphasizes care by and for the collective as well as by and for individuals.

Black feminist approaches to caring differ from their colorblind counterparts not only in closely considering issues of race, class, and culture, but in shifting the ethical and educational focus away from an idealized conception of caring to a more pragmatic model. Many mainstream theorists of caring hold that, in order to flourish, children and adolescents must be buffered from the alienating social order (Brown & Gilligan, 1992; Martin, 1992; Noddings, 1992; Taylor, Gilligan, & Sullivan, 1995). In the more pragmatic conception of caring found in the Black feminist literature, caregiving does not involve a retreat from conventional society "back to" some prior, more authentic, more innocent set of relations. Rather, it means promoting cultural integrity, communal and individual survival, spiritual growth, and political change under oppressive conditions (Cannon, 1988; Collins, 1990; Eugene, 1989; James, 1993).

Given that Black caregivers cannot prepare children to cope, let alone thrive, in a racist world by shielding them from all knowledge of that world, it is not innocence but knowledge that is at a premium in Black feminist caring. To prepare Black children to know themselves as Black, as part of a strong community, and as specifically *not* what a racist world would have them believe, their caregivers must start from the kind of powerful knowledge and mother-wit associated with communal elders. Thus, whereas colorblind caring often requires that the caregiver set aside her own needs and interests, so as to enter as fully as possible into the point of view of the individual child, in

Black feminist models of caring the caregiver proclaims the knowledge she shares with other strong Black women as a point of departure. In what Alice Walker (1983) calls "womanist" approaches to Black feminism, the woman takes charge; she is strong, competent, and responsible. To know and to change an unjust world, the womanist engages in "outrageous, audacious, courageous," and inquisitive behavior (p. xi).

Theme One: Authentic, Trustworthy Relationships

Because it celebrates childhood innocence, White child-centered teaching tends to suppress colortalk. For Black teachers of Black students, colortalk historically has been at the center of both knowledge and relationships (Foster, 1997; Siddle Walker, 1996). Recalling her childhood experiences of Black and White teachers, Bobbie Kirby (1998) remembers thinking that Black teachers "were not afraid to talk about anything, especially race." They turned racial incidents into moral, political, and academic lessons, "had the power to 'mess' in your life outside the classroom," and, in effect, "placed the fate of the whole race on your shoulders." By contrast, it seemed to her that White teachers "based their lessons on textbook materials," "were afraid to talk about controversial issues," and "wanted everybody to be the same" (p. 4). Both her Black and her White teachers tried to be caring. Yet they made very different assumptions about what would count as caring for children of color. Only her Black teachers acknowledged racism as an issue or used colortalk to help their students think about unjust and oppressive social relations.

In Black feminist writing, outspokenness and honest anger are crucial to trusting relations. While some White feminists may be made uncomfortable by any departure from niceness, the Black feminist literature has long insisted that trust between Blacks and Whites depends on Whites being able to hear Blacks' anger. Recalling a White woman who, in response to Lorde's anger, said, "'Tell me how you feel but don't say it too harshly or I cannot hear you'," Audre Lorde (1984) argues that anger must be expressed if it is to be a tool for change (p. 125). "Anger is loaded with information and energy," she says. Properly focused and "translated into action in the service of our vision," it "can become a powerful source of energy serving progress and change" (p. 127).

Taking White-Black relationships seriously, Lorde makes clear, means working through racial conflict, not glossing over or avoiding conflict in the name of niceness. Just as the suppression of colortalk forfeits the possibility of meaningful cross-race relationships by avoiding any acknowledgment of racial difference or conflict, the ladylike insistence on never showing anger forfeits the possibility of love, trust, and openness in the relationship. Too often, in mixed-race feminist groups, "the emphasis on providing care and support leads to White women's passive listening to diverse voices" and avoidance of "heated discussion or disagreement" (Razack, 1998, p. 50). When White women encounter disagreement from women of color, they may feel threatened and, as a result, disengage. But from a Black feminist perspective, naming oppression and whiteness is an *affirmation* of relationship. As African Canadian womanist Annette Henry (1995) puts it, raising "issues of power, oppression, and self-representation as marginalized people . . . is not an act of psychological bullying but rather an act of love and desire" (p. 16).

Colorblind models of caring that promote "playing nice" over telling the truth allow White women to remain comfortably oblivious to the racism in their own conduct. Schools commonly suppress colortalk on the grounds even mentioning race or racism promotes "divisiveness." Because the polite suppression of colortalk denies real conflict and real relationships, African American students—children as well as adolescents—may regard teachers' colortalk avoidance as a betrayal of trust (Christy, 1998). Some White students may share this perception. Lyn Brown (1998) has suggested that White adolescent girls distrust teachers and parents, especially women, who insist on glossing over conflict with niceness. A good teacher, girls told Brown, is one "who 'doesn't lie to us. She tells us the truth'" (p. 113).

Theme Two: A Black Standpoint

Just as White teachers' avoidance of any discussion of racism may erect a barrier to relationships with students of color, so too may their insistence on assuming that a White standpoint is neutral. Too often, the "universal" values claimed on behalf of White morality have been values that have served to rationalize and perpetuate inequality (Cannon, 1988; Chalmers, 1997; Woodson, 1933/1972). Speaking of White religious values, for example, Carter G. Woodson (1933/1972) wryly observed that insofar as these have been borrowed "from slaveholders, libertines, and murderers, there may be something wrong [with them], and it would not hurt to investigate" them (p. 73). In order to avoid the many blind spots and distortions in dominant White meaning codes, African Americans have had to develop ethical and epistemological positions predicated on their own experience, values, and sense of moral dignity (Cannon, 1988; Woodson, 1933/1972). Understanding Whiteness as well as Blackness and Brownness requires displacing Whiteness as the taken-for-granted center of knowledge and value.

Such a stance is distinctly at odds with the curriculum in U.S. and Canadian public schools, where discussions of White racism, Black history, and Black accomplishments in the arts and sciences are mostly notable by their absence (Castenell & Pinar, 1993; Jervis, 1996; Kelly, 1998). For example, "a survey of modern public school social studies texts reveals that the word *racism* does not appear in their indexes" (Kincheloe, 1993, p. 253), and no such textbook "examines the history of the northern urban Afro-American experience" (p. 254). In Alberta, a young Black man called Roy laments the paucity of information on Black historical figures. "I know about Booker T. Washington, that's obvious stuff but not others. . . . My parents started teaching me but that's the only place I can get" information on Blacks, he says (Kelly, 1998, p. 60).

Insofar as Black history is taken up in the curriculum, textbooks, and children's books, more often than not it is addressed in mystifying, ethnocentric, or stereotyped terms (Kincheloe, 1993; Kohl, 1995; Sims, 1982; Thompson, 2001). Fifteen-year-old Nadine, a Haitian, recounts how, "when I came here, all I learned about black culture in America was that black people were slaves, and then Martin Luther King showed up and single-handedly freed us all!" (Carroll, 1997, p. 123). Typically, the only aspect of Black history that is covered is slavery—with an emphasis on Black passivity (Kelly, 1998). "When they talk about us," Desmond says, "they talk about us being in chains. They don't talk about how we got out of it, what we did for ourselves" (Kelly, 1998, p. 130). Because Whiteness is assumed as the framework, Black culture and accomplishments are usually ignored. Even in discussions of Africa, the focus is on Black contact with Whites. As Desmond puts it, "When they talk about Africa, it's either because Africa is being invaded by another country or [about] apartheid" (p. 129).

When students ask their teachers for more information about African Americans and African Canadians, they are likely to be told that "we already did Black history last year." Shaka, who asked her social studies teacher for "something about black people," recalls that not only did the teacher get "mad," but all the students said "that I am a racist because I asked for a class on black stuff" (p. 132). Because White teachers rarely support Black students' requests for more attention to Black history, Black authors, or Black art and culture, young Black people are forced to educate themselves. As Grace says, "I have to go home and study and study so I can pass about someone else's culture and maybe if I have five minutes before I go to sleep I can . . . read about what I want to learn." "It does not seem fair," she says, that "we . . . have to learn all our history on our own time" (p. 133).

Colortalk decenters and denormalizes Whiteness, recognizing that a colorblind curriculum does not tell the truth about U.S. race relations. In showing young African Americans "where we came from" and "how we got over," culturally relevant and critically conscious education teaches students to cope with the racism they encounter every day on the street, in the media, in textbooks, and on the playground. For White students, learning Black history, learning the history of White racism, and unlearning deeply embedded cultural and political assumptions about White agency and Black passivity are crucial steps in undoing Whites' own mis-education.

Theme Three: A Pragmatic Orientation Toward Survival

"Contemporary African American communities," says Stanlie James (1993), "struggle around the dual themes of survival and social change," just as they have since slavery (p. 51). When "making a way out of no way" is simply a fact of life, children have to be taught not only how to cope but also how to set about fostering political, institutional, and social change. Accordingly, the Black family gives "the child criteria for determining malice" when confronted with racism and helps "the child determine what action was then appropriate for retribution or reconciliation" (Ward, 1990, p. 223). Struggling to negotiate the right balance between protection from and preparation for the racism of the social order (King & Mitchell, 1995), Black mothers cannot simply retreat to the private sphere but must prepare their children for an often hostile public sphere. Far from trying to protect childish innocence, then, African American mothers, teachers, and othermothers usually seek to alert young people to the various threats to their survival and flourishing, so as to help them learn to respond to racism and sexism productively and without loss of integrity.

Given the situations of Black women and their families, conventional, White, middle- and upper-class, feminine values are "non-functional in the pragmatic survival lifestyle of Black women" (Cannon, 1988, p. 125). As Collins (1990) notes, the caring work of the Black mother may be too laborious to allow time or energy for the kind of affectionate display that is associated with mothering in the dominant culture. Nevertheless, sheer physical, wage-earning and homemaking labor is "an act of love," a commitment to the survival and flourishing of one's children (p. 129). As June Jordan (1985) recalls of her own mother, "her way of offering love" was to work endless hours in an effort to offer her daughter "a reliable home base where I could pursue the privileges of books and music." Such women's sacrifice and "the humility of their love" make possible "the dream of freedom" that their children can then pursue (p. 105). Rather than grounding virtues in a freestanding ethical ideal, Black feminist traditions base them in a pragmatic vision of the possible. While changing what is possible is also part of that vision, survival is at times a more pressing concern.

Emphasizing the pragmatic aspects of caring in African American traditions does not authorize a deficit reading of Black mothering. As bell hooks (1990) points out, if focusing on the cruelty of slave conditions that "separated black families, black mothers from their children" leads us to see only what Black mothers could *not* give their children—leads us to focus, for example, on enslaved mothers' inability to shower their children with the constant affection associated with the White ideal of motherhood—then we fail to see "the quality of care" that led Frederick Douglass's enslaved mother to walk 12 miles at night to hold her young son until he fell asleep (p. 44). Assuming a supposedly generic maternal ideal and then reading the oppressive conditions under which Black mothers have had to labor as excusing or explaining away a failure to achieve this maternal ideal obscures the creativity and richness of the caring values characteristic of Black feminist traditions. Thus, the African American tradition of othermothering, in which female relatives and other women share child-care responsibilities with a child's mother, is misread if it is understood simply as an adaptation to economic and oppressive conditions that prevent birth mothers from being fully available to their children. Othermothering is not a fallback option, to be used if the nuclear-family ideal is unattainable, but a valued caring tradition that enriches the lives of children while also strengthening the communal kin relations between adults (Collins, 1990; hooks, 1984; James, 1993; Ward, 1995).

Theme Four: Exploitative and Oppressive Social Relations

Given that, historically, Blacks' situation has not remotely resembled the ideal assumed in White ethical traditions, Black feminist ethics holds that it is impossible to separate questions of ethics from situational considerations (Cannon, 1988). Most White justice and caring theorists, by contrast, specifically reference ethics to an ideal. The former appeal to principled justice as the ideal by which ethical and political relations are to be evaluated (e.g., Kohlberg, 1981); the latter usually appeal to an ideal referenced either to the domestic sphere (e.g., Martin, 1992) or to mothering (e.g., Noddings, 1992). Mainstream (usually, but not always White) theorists of caring who reject conventionally feminine social ideals of caring tend to invoke some other, purportedly more natural, ideal in their place. Brown (1998), Brown and Gilligan (1992), and Taylor, Gilligan, and Sullivan (1995), for example, appeal to girls' presocialized, childhood instincts about relationships as a more authentic relational orientation than the kind of caring associated with the pure, self-sacrificing woman.

The idealism, individualism, and colorblindness of White ethical and educational traditions contrasts markedly with the political and communal pragmatism of Black traditions of justice and caring. Making no bones about the importance of recognizing and struggling against racism, generations of Black teachers in all-Black settings have reminded their students that they need to do twice as well as their White counterparts if they are to succeed in a White, racist society (Foster, 1997; Siddle Walker, 1996). They have warned students about buying into racist language and assumptions, have taught them about the historical struggles and achievements of Black people, and have urged them to "lift" as they "climb." Colortalk—understood as part of the curriculum as well as part of what it means to look out for one's students—has played a key role in what it means to teach.

Black child-centered education thus takes a very different form from its White counterpart. In mainstream child-centered education, attending to the whole child means affirming and expanding the child's authentic, innocent stance toward the world, while refraining from imposing adult knowledge on the child. But in Black traditions of caring and education, caring for the whole child is likely to include concern for the child's cultural and political growth. As Vanessa Siddle Walker (1996) shows us in her study of a segregated Black school, the teachers and school principal recognized their students as political and civic beings who needed to learn to understand the world in the way that Black adults do. Although Siddle Walker invokes the traditional language of child-centered education, she shows us that what the "whole child" *meant* to teachers included the child in her or his political and communal capacity.

CONCLUSION: CARE REQUIRES ABANDONING COLORBLINDNESS FOR COLORTALK

Wanting to protect childhood innocence is an undeniable temptation for caring parents and teachers—Black as well as White. Under slavery, Black families and communities extended as much protection as they could to their children; wherever possible, they sought to buffer children from the brutal conditions ahead of them. Thus, "children were never 'lowed to stay round grown folks when they was talkin,'" both because the children might overhear and repeat dangerous slave secrets and because the adults wanted to preserve the children's innocence as long as possible (Clayton, 1990, p. 197). To protect children while also keeping them ignorant, Black adults were forced to be extremely strict. Since children ignorant of the brutality of slavery naturally would not understand the danger from Whites if they failed to behave according to the established racist codes, Black parents had to demand unquestioning obedience from their children. Any deviation from absolute obedience spelled enormous danger both for the child and for the family and community. Ironically, then, protecting childhood innocence—a kind of caring that, in contemporary educational thought, is usually associated with gentleness and a fair degree of indulgence—was made possible only by a highly authoritarian parentchild relation.

Under slavery, Black childhood innocence could not last for long. By the time Black children were 5 or 6, slaveowners put them to work. The children would then need to be taught how to survive—and how to resist. Today, African American children still must be taught by their families and communities how to cope with racism and how to resist oppression. Black children cannot afford to be innocent and cannot afford to trust teachers who pretend that racism is not real. Culturally conscious picture books such as *Tar Beach* show us some of the complexity of Black childhood in a racist society (Sims, 1982; Thompson, 2001). Whereas colorblind educational theories commonly insist upon innocence and ignorance as the universal (and appropriate) condition of childhood, *Tar Beach* allows us to see children as knowers—as observant of, thoughtful about, and responsive to the injustice of a racist social order.

Teaching African American second graders many years ago, Patricia Hill Collins (1998) realized that, in uncritically using a textbook full of statements such as "the policeman is your friend," she was lying to her students (p. ix). Cops rarely visit Black neighborhoods to protect African Americans; they usually show up only when they are looking to arrest a Black person. Phrases such as "the policeman is your friend" are articulated to a White, not a Black, world. Her students' education began only when Collins asked them to think critically about the contradictions between the nice, safe world portrayed in their textbook and the real world they knew in their own everyday lives.

For White teachers who know little about the everyday experience of race and racism, the challenge in caring for Black students and other students of color is to *see* the world that the children see, and to help them develop thoughtful responses both to cultural difference and to racism (see chapter 2). It is a responsibility owed to White students as well. We cannot prepare children to make a better world if we cannot see *this* world for what it is. In recent years, the biblical saying, "I was blind, but now I see" (John 9:25), has been invoked in a new form: "Was colorblind, but now I see." To truly see White, Black, and Brown relations in a raced and racist society—both as they are and as they might be—we must care enough to abandon our willed ignorance and political blindness.

CHAPTER 2

The Play of Voices:
Black Adolescents Constituting
the Self and Morality

Garrett Albert Duncan

> We, the Blacks, are in trouble, certainly, but we are not inarticulate
> because we are not compelled to defend a morality that we know to be
> a lie.
>
> —James Baldwin, *On Prejudice*

CAROL GILLIGAN's study of women calls attention to "different ways of constituting the self and morality" (1986b, p. 325).
The study of Black culture and life in the United States also provides
unique insights into the construction of the self and morality for
Black adolescents. Indeed, the social, cultural, and ideological sources
that shape Black people's lives and experiences position them to articulate important narratives that counter traditional views on justice
and care. Yet, as James Baldwin suggests in the preceding epigraph,
those in positions to name and construct social reality often characterize Black people as inarticulate. This is especially true when Black
people expose institutional lies and reveal how dominant narratives, including those on morality, are constructed in the interests
of White supremacy. More often than not, these voices are silenced,
and the people who articulate them are rendered invisible and excluded from meaningful participation in the social construction of reality.

In this chapter, I will interweave concepts drawn from identity
and moral development research to explore theoretically the ways in

which the study of Black adolescence contributes to our understanding of morality in the United States. My discussion is grounded in data from interviews I conducted with Black youth and supplemented with autobiographical and other literary sources. Together, these sources allow me to expand the traditional approaches to moral functioning, to portray real-life morality in the lived experiences of Black youth, and to connect these voices to those of other Africans in America who have also asserted their humanity under dehumanizing moral dilemmas.

THEORETICAL CONSIDERATIONS

"The play of voices" in this chapter's title describes the complexity of the response patterns that Black youth use to mediate, reconcile, and integrate their lived experiences with the broader society, especially the dilemmas they encounter in their day-to-day interactions. This approach rejects the view that Black youth are rootless, that they exist apart from a larger Black culture, and that they have no sense of historical context. Instead, it conveys the sense that any number of cultural tools inform all utterances and that all utterances simultaneously echo and respond directly and indirectly to other utterances. To elucidate their worlds in this manner, I draw upon two theoretical terms: *bicultural moral voices*, and *diasporan and ethnic voices*.

Bicultural Moral Voices

A growing body of research emphasizes the complexity of sociocultural processes among African Americans (e.g., Barnes, 1972; Billingsley, 1973, 1992; Cross, 1991; Duncan, 1993, 1996, 2000; Fordham, 1996; Kelley, 1997; Mama, 1995; Spencer, 1988, 1999; Ward, 2000). For the purpose of this chapter, I will focus on the research literature on bicultural development. Biculturalism is a process wherein individuals function in two distinct sociocultural milieus, their primary culture of origin and that of the dominant society in which they live (Darder, 1991). The research tradition on biculturalism is rich and varied (see, for example, Akinyela, 2003; Darder, 1991, 1995; deAnda, 1984; Ramirez & Castenada, 1974; Rashid, 1984; Valentine, 1971). Models of bicultural development emphasize "a mechanism of survival that constitutes forms of adaptive alternatives in the face of hegemonic control and institutional oppression." Further, these alternatives must be understood as forms of resistance that may or may not "function in the emancipatory interest of the individuals who utilize them in their lives" (Darder, 1991, p. 49).

Antonia Darder (1991) describes four major bicultural response patterns: alienation, dualism, separatism, and negotiation. *Cultural alienation* reflects responses in which an individual identifies with the dominant culture and rejects identification with the primary culture. *Cultural dualism* is characteristic of those individuals who maintain separate identities, one that allows acceptance in the primary culture and another that allows acceptance in the dominant culture. *Cultural separation* describes how individuals remain entirely within the primary culture and adamantly reject the dominant culture. *Cultural negotiation*, finally, describes the process by which individuals seek to referee, reconcile, and integrate their lived experiences in ways that honor the integrity of their primary cultural identity, while working to socially transform the society at large.

Darder considers these response patterns in terms of the extent to which they support *bicultural affirmation*, which involves the self that W. E. B. Du Bois (1903) described as the merging of the "double self into a better and truer self" within which "neither of the older selves [is] lost" (p. 3). Bicultural affirmation informs the capacity of individuals to transform social structures in the direction of a more culturally democratic and socially just society (cf. Banks, 2002). According to Darder, both alienated and separatist responses, insofar as they engage one cultural identity to the exclusion of the other, move individuals away from bicultural affirmation; in contrast, dualist and negotiated responses, which more or less engage both cultural identities, move them toward bicultural affirmation.

In Darder's (1991) view, "Bicultural affirmation response patterns may hold the greatest emancipatory possibility in respect to the struggle for cultural democracy in the schools" (p. 57). He supports this premise despite the fact that movement in the direction of bicultural affirmation does not necessarily result in the emancipatory interests of the individual being served because the social conditions remain unchanged. I would also suggest that movement *away* from bicultural affirmation toward alienation or separation does not necessarily work *against* the emancipatory interests of individuals either. As Martin Luther King Jr. indicated in remarks he made during a rabbinical conference only days before he was assassinated, in a racist society, separatism may function as a strategic, temporary move in the direction of personal and social liberation, which are preconditions of any integrated society, especially those that are culturally democratic (King, 1967c, 1986).

Diasporan and Ethnic Voices

The use of the term *diasporan African voices* indicates that Black culture in the United States has part of its origin in the experiences of captive or displaced Africans whose descendants never have been fully integrated or accepted into the mainstream of American culture. These voices sometimes conflict with what I call *ethnic American voices*. As cultural tools, some ethnic American voices are tinged with what Toni Morrison (1992) calls a "carefully invented Africanist presence" (p. 6), those understandings that fortify a manner of seeing the world in ways that serve the interests of White individuals and groups, whom we tacitly understand to be normal, and that denigrate people of color, whom we understand to be inferior or of marginal status.

The distinction between diasporan and ethnic voices is mainly analytic in that it is useful to highlight the specific tools that youth use to make meaning of their lives that contrast with those that dominant institutions distribute throughout society (Noddings, 1995). What distinguishes diasporan African voices from conventional voices of justice and care is that the former are transmitted via cultural narratives that have been fashioned within the historical context of the Black diaspora in North America. They reflect the values and social norms of a community and come to bear in mediating personal and social dilemmas, and thus they function as "moral" voices (Ladner, 1973; Garrod, Ward, Robinson, & Kilkenny, 1999; Gwaltney, 1980; Ture & Hamilton, 1992).

THREE DIASPORAN AFRICAN VOICES

In what follows, I will provide an overview of the voices of 22 Black adolescents in California, 13 young women and 9 young men (Figure 4). Interviews were conducted with these Black youth in settings they chose to access the complexity inherent in Black perspectives of identity and morality (for details regarding the research procedure, see Duncan, 2002). The general diasporan voice can be heard in the following student's remarks:

> Since we were brought here on ships, we were called different things—and it's like an evolution. We started as being niggers or nigra. . . . They always classified us as what *they* thought we were: what we looked like, how we wore our hair, the color of our skin. Now we are African Americans, saying that we were

FIGURE 4. Participant Profiles

Student	Gender	Age	Religious Identity	Racial Identity	Parents' Occupation(s)
Patricia	Female	13	Christian	African American	Semiskilled workers
Albert	Male	14	Christian	African American	Semiprofessionals
Roni	Female	14	Baptist		Semiprofessional
Louis	Male	15	Christian	African American	Semiprofessionals
Paige	Female	15	Baptist	Black	Skilled worker
Clayton	Male	16	Islam	Black	Unknown
Daniel	Male	16	Ma'at	African	Professional
David	Male	16		African	Professionals
Grace	Female	16	Adventist	Black and White	Semiprofessional (father); semiskilled worker (mother)
Melvin	Male	16	Jehovah's Witness	Black	Unemployed
Clifton	Male	17	Baptist	Black	Semiprofessional (father); clerical (mother)
Darla	Female	17	Presbyterian	African American	Semiprofessional
Gina	Female	17	Pentecostal	African American	Semiskilled workers
Irene	Female	17	Adventist	Black	Professional (father); semiprofessional (mother)
Kwesi	Male	17		African/ Black	Professional (mother); skilled worker (father)
Monica	Female	17	Believes in God	Black	Semiprofessionals
Regina	Female	17	Christian	African	Professional
Temika	Female	17	AME (African Methodist Episcopal)	Black	Semiprofessionals
Louise	Female	18		African	Professional
Kenyah	Male	18	Christian	Black	Semiprofessionals
Veronica	Female	18	Baptist	African	Skilled worker (mother); unskilled worker (father)
Brenda	Female	20	Christian	Black	Semiprofessionals

Note: All names are pseudonyms. Parents' occupational ratings are based the Hollingshead Occupational Index (Hollingshead, 1975), which was adapted by combining minor, lesser, and major "professional" occupations into one category.

first Africans, but now since we are over here, we're Americans.
Well, I was never asked to be brought over here, so I will never
consider myself to be an American. . . . So I title myself African.
(Kwesi)

These interviews led me to identify three conjunctive sets of diasporan African voices within a framework that expresses perspectives
that affirm Black life and culture: *subordinate-subjugated* voices, *unofficial-underground* voices, and *transgressive-profane* voices. I describe and analyze these voices in terms of their "positions" relative
to dominant discourses.

Subordinate-Subjugated Voices

Subordinate-subjugated voices refute racist imagery implicit in the everyday moral discourse that most people take for granted. Such imagery is conveyed through benign metaphors such as *minorities, under-
class, underprivileged,* and *at-risk*—terms most people use without
second thoughts that, in effect, convey racialized imagery. Subordinate-subjugated voices reveal at the most basic level that Black people
know that they are normal in a society that represents them as abnormal. These voices also may respond directly to racist institutional
constructions of Black culture. For example, Othman Sullivan, an in-
formant in Gwaltney's (1980) postcolonial ethnography *Drylongso,*
mused aloud, "I think this anthropology is just another way to call me
a nigger" (p. xix). Likewise, Langston Hughes (1969) resonates these
perspectives when he laments, "Misery is when you heard on the radio that the neighborhood you live in is a slum but you always thought
it was home" (p. 1). To the extent that these voices refute notions
of ontological blackness, or "the blackness that Whiteness created"
(Anderson, 1995, p. 13), they are ethical. More plainly, these voices
allow the speaker to reclaim standing within the boundaries of a community within which moral values, concepts of beauty, and truth considerations apply without respect to cultural or ancestral heritage
(Ward, 1991).

Like Sullivan and Hughes, the Black youth in my study were
quick to point out the social fabrications that serve to dehumanize
them. For example, Veronica, age 18, deconstructed what it is to be
female, feminine, and beautiful in the context of U.S. society. Speaking of her perception of how she looked to others, Veronica noted:

A woman is supposed to be quite feminine and very ladylike and
dainty. And can't have any blemishes and must be perfect and

prissy. That's not me. Like the song, "I may not be a lady but I am all woman." I don't have to be makeup down, have on some high heels and some stockings, and a fancy dress to be a woman. I think that though society says that I have to, but society says I also have to be "blond and blue eyed." The more you want me to be blond hair and blue eyes, the more I'm going to say that I'm the sun and cut all my hair off.

Providing a similar perspective, 17-year-old Kwesi stated:

In this society, we are taught that we must fit in, from since we were little kids, by the fact that their skin is beautiful, the little butts, little thighs, blond hair and blue eyes—the Barbie doll effect. So [girls] are taught that you don't look like that, with the long hair and all beautiful. That's because, to fit in, it makes you want to look similar to that. But I don't agree with that; I do not think it's necessary. People should be individuals.

Both Kwesi's and Veronica's responses may be understood in a number of ways. Clearly, "fitting in" is characteristic of the general experience of adolescents in which young people grapple with adult society's expectations of conformity and their own desires for self-definition. Noddings (2002), for instance, posits that there is a direct relationship between youth's experience of care and their desire to be accepted: "The desire for acceptability . . . invites encounters that may themselves be caring or may lead to relations of care . . . a society depends on [the desire for acceptability] for ceremonies, routines, and scripts of all sorts" (p. 190). At the same time, one can sense from Kwesi's response that "fitting in" requires a greater sacrifice on the part of Black communities, a sacrifice that neither begins nor ends with the period of adolescence. How to negotiate these sacrifices is the stuff of the critical lessons and stories that inform the cultural milieus of Black children and youth.

These critical lessons, however, can take on different forms. In some instances, they foster cultural negotiation, and in others, cultural dualism or cultural separatism. Sixteen-year-old Clayton's remarks, like those of Veronica, reflect the latter as he describes both his awareness and rejection of society's standards. Describing a situation in which he felt he could not be himself, he reports:

I was on my way to the dentist and was told [by a member of my family] that "White people won't accept you if you look that way." And I didn't understand, so I was like, you know, "I'm really not trying to please them. My life on this earth is not to show and prove to White people who I am," you know what I'm saying? I don't have to justify my existence to *them*. I have to justify my existence because *everything* has to justify its existence—animals, everything.

Veronica and Kwesi respond to broader, more generalized "conversations" that permeate the discourse on beauty in the United States. Clayton's comments refer to his direct experiences and make explicit reference to White people while engaging a larger, "silent" conversation on double consciousness. He rejects the prescriptions of the larger White society, even when they are conveyed through the precautions of a family member.

Albert, age 14, and his 15-year-old brother, Louis, made observations regarding public life that were similar to Clayton's. Although they have personal standards of respectability that are different from those of the dominant White society, the brothers are especially aware of their bodies and language when in public, reflecting the double consciousness that referees their day-to-day experiences. When asked to describe situations in which they feel that they cannot be themselves, the brothers replied:

> *Albert*: I'll say I'm different around—I'm not a racist or nothing—I'm different around other races, you know. Around other non-Blacks, you know. . . . I'm myself when I'm around, like . . .
>
> *Louis*: Blacks?
>
> *Albert*: Blacks, yeah [laughter]. Whites, you know, try to stereotype, you know, most of the time. I try to make it so they won't think that—we are not all bad. Some of us are pretty good.
>
> *Garrett*: So, does this include when you're at school? When you're in the store?
>
> *Albert*: The store, mainly, yes. You try to be more intelligent so they don't think you're a stupid nigger.
>
> *Louis*: Like you don't walk how you usually walk when you with somebody else.
>
> *Albert*: And you talk more intelligent, don't just say half the word, say the whole word, you know.

Albert and Louis echo the insights of the postcolonial theorist Frantz Fanon (1967), who, more than 30 years ago, lamented, "Yes, I must take great pains with my speech, because I shall be more or less judged by it" (p. 20). However, their words also emphasize that the experiences of oppression of Blacks in America continue to profoundly influence present behavior. Albert, for example, added, "People look at me like I'm not all that smart" and that he therefore at times behaves in ways that fulfill their expectations. He surmised that, despite how he behaves, White people will never extend to him the respect that he is due as a human being; Louis affirms his brother's comments, noting that these perceptions are "stereotypes; they are bad concepts."

Despite obstacles, Black adolescents sometimes reject these stereotypes against their humanity, even when such resistance places them in harm's way. For instance, after Kwesi had helped a White child in his neighborhood who had fallen from her tricycle, he was detained by police officers who were patrolling the area. The officers released Kwesi only after White adult witnesses verified that he had not assaulted the little girl. In retrospect, Kwesi conceded that when he saw the child on the ground, he initially hesitated and even considered turning the other way, anticipating the danger to which he would expose himself by helping the young child. Here, Kwesi was caught in a dilemma of care of self and care of others. This dilemma "vies with the tendency toward exclusion expressed in the moral opposition between selfish and selfless choice—an opposition where selfishness connotes the exclusion of others and selflessness the exclusion of the self" (Gilligan, 1986a, p. 293). In other words, Kwesi could choose to help the child and risk a violent confrontation with adults who seek to continue to oppress, possibly even police officers. Or he could avoid such a risk, abandon the child, and protect his own self-interests. In confronting this scenario, Kwesi exemplifies the dilemma inherent in the subordinate-subjugated voices: Despite being treated as though he is abnormal, he responds in a way that demonstrates and affirms his humanity.

Unofficial-Underground Voices

Unofficial-underground voices refute official versions of both past and present events. Unofficial knowledge is transmitted through the lessons of critical consciousness, the "grapevine," and other "underground" sources, such as alternative magazines, Black-oriented radio stations, and "revisionist" texts that directly refute versions of events as conveyed through "mainstream" media. For example, when the question is asked whether the Black Panther Party is a terrorist organization or a constructive force in Black communities, unofficial-underground voices suggest the latter. Psychologist Erik Erikson also saw this, for instance, when he drew a similar comparison between the Black Panthers and Mahatma Gandhi (Erikson & Newton, 1973). Unofficial-underground voices, that is, become moral voices by turning conventional "truth" on its head. These voices challenge the normalcy of White supremacy in the past and present by providing alternative testimonials and versions of reality.

Unofficial and underground voices directly relate to how Black adolescents engage the politics of race and ethnicity in the United States. Race, in this sense, is a force that separates and emphasizes differences; ethnicity, in contrast, is a force that unifies and brings together disparate elements. Along these lines, although Black youth honor ethnic voices connecting them to other Americans, they at the same time honor their diasporan heritage. This became evident in the ways in which they identified themselves as members of U.S. society. I asked them what term they used to identify themselves in society because of differences I anticipated between the use of the ethnic signifier *African American* in the news and academic settings and the use of the racial signifier *Black* in settings, such as at home, in the community, and in public school classrooms.

The adolescents I interviewed labeled themselves as Black (41%), African (23%), African American (23%), African/Black (5%), or biracial Black and White (5%). Like most Africans in America, they most often called themselves Black, compared to the other four categories, and generally rejected the *hyphenated* term African-American (Alexander, 1992; Hecht, Collier, & Ribeau, 1993; Office of Management and Budget [OMB], 1997; Parham & Williams, 1993). The reasons for this vary, but as a number of youth whom I interviewed suggested, at least one reason may be their rejection of efforts by the larger society to level the perception of diversity and to gloss over testy questions of race and ethnicity in the United States. Seventeen-year-old Temika, who was emphatic in her reference to herself as a Black woman, captured this sentiment. When asked if she would call herself anything other than Black, she replied:

> No. I'm not too keen to African-American. [*Why?*] Because, that's just like, you know, Asian-American, *African*-American— what's another one?—Mexican-American. That's just a label— that's just what they are allowed to say on the news. (You know what they really want to call us.) I would rather not even get into that, "We're just African-Americans." No!

Temika suggested that the prescriptive labels that regulate official knowledge barely mask the contempt that the mainstream media express for people of color in their depictions of them. On the one hand, the media regularly refer to people of color as Americans, but on the other hand, as Temika said, "you know what they really want to call us." Temika's preceding utterance by definition contains an unofficial-underground voice insofar as it responds to and refutes the official knowledge contained in a mainstream account of social reality.

The strident criticism and rejection of certain things American by some of these students—as exemplified in the refusal of 41% of them to accept the more ethnic signifier *African American*—by no means has gone uncontested by their teachers and peers. Yet, as Louise indicates, conscious adolescents are usually ready for the task of defending their positions. Along these lines, the 18-year-old shared the following story:

> Me and Darrin Smith, from the seventh grade on up, we used to get into arguments. I said, "I hate America, like I want to go back to Africa." And he's like, "I've been to Africa and in Zimbabwe" and this and that. "It's horrible and you wouldn't want to live there and they'd consider you a stupid American," all this stuff. And we went head up, because he felt one way about Africa, and I felt one way about Africa, and we both had been there.
>
> I don't know; it's like America puts on this facade and says that they're doing everything to help everybody. They're like the godmother to the world and they're there to help. And I just couldn't stand it. Once you start hearing what's really going on behind closed doors.

Adolescents who reject the hyphenated term *African-American* also give reasons that refer to issues of domination, imperialism, and coercion and that have little to do with "racial pride" and "ethnic boosterism."

Certainly, some Black youth also quite readily identify themselves as American. For example, 16-year-old Melvin identified himself as "Black or African American." In fact, Melvin noted that labels are not that important to him: "Really, I identify myself as American because I'm in America. I was born in America, so I'm like, I'm American." However, he stressed that it is important for him to be designated as a *Black* American. Melvin continued:

> Well, you know, like your family, when they tell you stories, your grandmother and your grandfather, they give you stories.

And then you learn through school. It's like some struggles you might go through because of, like, your nationality or whatever. Really, it's like things you have experienced. And then you see yourself in the mirror.

Whether the youth accept the term *African American* or reject it, most of the adolescents who take issue with their status as Americans do not do so in a vacuum and are not unlike the individuals depicted in *Drylongso* (Gwaltney, 1980). For example, John Oliver, characterized by his community as a "generous, judicious person who merits the generosity and respect of others" (p. 15), had this to say about the issue:

> I get tired of that one-nation-under-God boogie-woogie. We are ourselves. We are our *own* nation or country or whatever you want to call it. We are no one-tenth of some White something! That man has got his country and we *are* our country. Maybe we might get to that one nation, but we sure won't make it the way we're going now! If the Lord took every White . . . away this afternoon, it wouldn't change me any. We don't need them to do what we do. They need us more than we need them. How many Black people have you ever heard come on with that one-nation stuff? (p. 19)

Black adolescents, echoing the critical lessons of the stories told to them by their immediate families and communities, are diverse and offer multiple perspectives of what it means to be American. Many of these voices make specific references to unofficial-underground accounts about the society at large that challenge dominant liberal and conservative narratives. In addition to those passed along by family members, students often refer to the critical lessons they learned from others in local and national Black communities.

Transgressive-Profane Voices

Transgressive-profane diasporan African voices, elements of which were also included in the preceding examples, are voices that respond indirectly to mainstream narrative discourses in history, religion, and culture and, given their reliance upon metaphors, may or may not be comprehensible to most Americans. These voices, like others, have explicit and hidden communication characteristics. Also, as suggested earlier, unofficial-underground voices that advance alternative views of American institutions often underlie these critiques.

I identify transgressive voices as such because they provide alternatives to, and go against the grain of, the knowledge generated by dominant institutions. They are also profane because they critique these institutions with a considerable degree of contempt and outrage, as indicated by the strong, sometimes blasphemous, language that individuals use to make their point. An interview with Frederick Douglass, abolitionist, freedom fighter, and major critic of the practice of Christianity, for example, referred to White people as "devils." Because of the tone of his statements on religion, those who did not know him might suppose he was opposed to all religion. Thus, Douglass (1845) clarified his position:

> What I have said respecting and against religion, I mean strictly to apply to the *slaveholding religion* of this land, and with no possible reference to Christianity proper; for, between the Christianity of this land, and the Christianity of Christ, I recognize the widest possible difference—so wide, that to receive one as good, pure, and holy, is of necessity to reject the other as bad, corrupt, and wicked.—I love the pure peaceable and impartial Christianity of Christ: I therefore hate the corrupt, slaveholding, women-whipping, cradle-plundering, partial and hypocritical Christianity of this land. (p. 120)

Adolescents use transgressive-profane voices as cultural tools that, like Douglass, explicitly challenge some of the core values of United States society, especially as these are disseminated through its major institutions, such as schools, religious institutions, government agencies, and the news media.

Transgressive-profane voices grab hold of what it means to be an American and, at times, what it means to be human in ways that contravene and disrespect mainstream views. Some young Black males, for instance, refer to themselves as God (Duncan, 1996), and the meanings attributed to God are at variance with how most people in this country have historically conceived of God. Further, these ideas are promulgated within organizations that have marginal and often outlaw status in the United States, such as the Nation of Islam and the Five Percent Nation of Poor, Righteous Teachers as well as organizations such as the Universal Negro Improvement Association, the Black Panther Party for Self-Defense, the Association for the Study of Classical African Civilizations, the New Afrikan Independent Movement, and Us, to name just a few. Transgressive-profane voices, however, are not the sole property of such organizations. In addition, transgressive-profane voices have been appropriated and circulated in the work of a number of rap artists and hip-hop icons, including Kool Moe Dee, Public Enemy, KRS-One, Arrested Development, and recently, Erika Badu and Lauryn Hill. Moreover, Black teenagers have developed these voices also to articulate truths that respond to forms of disparagement that are specific to youth cultures in the United States. For example, Kwesi recounted the following episode at school that elicited these voices.

> I tell everybody that I believe that I am God. But, before, I used to say I never believed in God. They would be like "Kwesi, are you a Christian?" And I would say "no" that I'm not. "Well, what religion are you?" I'd say, "I'm my own religion." They would say, "Do you believe in God?" Right then and there I had to hesitate. . . . And they said, "You don't believe in God?!" And that just changed the whole subject right there. And they were going off! . . . Then the teacher sent me to the office.

Reporting that his parents had received calls from school because he rejected Christianity and saw himself as his "own religion," Kwesi went on to recount how his attitudes were specifically at odds with the curriculum at school:

> My second period, we were doing our report. I think it was a history report—and one part of this book said that Marcus Garvey seemed to be a Black Moses. And I had comments about that—a lot. I mean, I didn't agree with that. I thought that Moses was Black himself. So, as soon as I said that, a lot of hands raised.
>
> But the thing about God, in each one of my periods, it's like, "You don't believe in God? You believe that you're God? I don't think so—you ain't perfect and this and this and this." But especially in first period, they called me into the office and stuff. And I've had threats and stuff, like "You're going to hell" and "I can't wait for the devil to get a hold of you." I'd say, "What, the White man?" And they all look puzzled and go "What?" And then, most of the people, when I talk like that, they say, "You must be Muslim or something." I mean, I've been to the mosque and stuff, but I'm not Muslim. And "you a militant nigger, huh?" And this and that. But it's all right.

The transgressive-profane voice of Kwesi, and its rejection by society, can also be identified in the 1995 case of a teacher who was fired from her position in the Ferguson-Florrisant School District in St. Louis County, Missouri, for allowing her mainly Black students to use "profanity" on a videotaped creative writing assignment. The teacher was removed once again from her position by a judge who overturned a jury verdict that reinstated the teacher to her job and awarded her punitive damages of $750,000. Among the issues that the case highlighted were those of adolescent voices and whether the teacher's assignment had instructional merit or simply encouraged attitudes and behaviors that undermined student academic achievement. Implicitly, the transgressive-profane voices of the adolescents were deemed inappropriate and in conflict with the mainstream views of the school. These themes are also at the heart of educational controversies, such as those surrounding the use of Alice Walker's (1992) *The Color Purple* in public schools or as captured in John Henrik Clarke's (1966) classic short story, "The Boy Who Painted Christ Black."

Unlike other diasporan African voices, transgressive-profane voices have solid associations with groups with marginal and outlaw status in society. As such, these voices incorporate themselves rather uneasily into different settings, as illustrated by Kwesi's examples. In addition, these voices are subject to criticisms ranging from the mild to severe within dominant institutions, such as public schools and academic and research settings (Arendt, 1970; Kohlberg, 1981). Indeed, these voices are also subject to sanctions by groups and individuals within Black communities. Thus, although subordinated-subjugated voices and unofficial-underground voices pepper the stories and critical lessons that circulate throughout Black communities, transgressive-profane voices have a much more limited distribution in society.

CONCLUSION: FOSTER BICULTURAL AFFIRMATION AMONG BLACK STUDENTS

Before outlining what I believe to be the implications of the preceding discussion for moral education, I want to reiterate that, although I highlight certain undertheorized dimensions of adolescent experience, Black teenagers experience multiple life-worlds, including those related to youth cultures as well as a larger Black culture (Garrod, Smulyan, Powers, & Kilkenny, 2002). Like other adolescents, Black youths experience a "metamorphosis," as Louise explained in her "description of herself" to herself, and their identity development occurs within the context of a biologically based life cycle shared by youths of all backgrounds (Erikson & Newton, 1973). But Black adolescents also frame moral situations in terms of resistance to oppression and a legacy of Black struggle for equality.

As I see it, two interlocking implications for moral education are suggested by this study that relate to bicultural affirmation (Darder, 1991) and that are consistent with the aims of moral research and education to cultivate the voices of young people (Gilligan, 1986a). First, bicultural affirmation fosters within Black students the psychological conditions wherein "assimilation, imitation, or assuming the role of the rebellious exotic other are not the only available options" for them in public school (hooks, 1990, p. 20). It also allows them to merge the "double self into a better and truer self" within which "neither of the older selves [is] lost" (Du Bois, 1903, p. 3). Second, along these lines, fostering the conditions that promote bicultural affirmation among Black students has both ethical and curricular implications.

From an ethical standpoint, promoting and sustaining the conditions that foster bicultural affirmation of Black students require that teachers recognize and affirm that classrooms are relatively autonomous places that provide contexts in which to nurture forms of expression that we usually silence and discourage in our youths. The adolescents spoke highly of teachers, albeit a precious few, who created spaces within classrooms where students could express themselves and, at the same time, where these teachers affirmed *and* challenged the viewpoints of their students. Here, these teachers understood that adolescent voices, like all voices, are complex and contradictory and that nurturing these voices meant doing so with purpose. Given that voices incorporate a range of conflicting and contradictory impulses, both reflecting and refracting the images of a racist and sexist society, such aspects of adolescent voices are inevitable, and these teachers directly engaged them. For example, some Black youth resist academic work, designating such activity as meaningless and irrelevant, even labeling it as a form of "acting White" (cf. Spencer, Noll, Stoltzfus, & Harpalani, 2001) According to the participants in my study, these teachers did not negotiate with students when it came to doing academic work, regardless of the subject matter.

Perhaps most important, the teenagers reported that these teachers avoided the permissiveness that characterizes the classrooms where their compassionate and well-intentioned peers fail to make critical distinctions between forms of student resistance that critique oppression and those that undermine the students' own human dignity. As it relates to a pedagogy that is informed by ethical commitments, the teachers they described moved beyond caring as simply a sentimental or sympathetic feeling and embraced it as a process that engaged conflict and disagreement and that manifested itself in action (Blizek, 1999; Delpit, 1995; Eaker-Rich & Van Galen, 1996; hooks, 2000; Siddle Walker, 1996).

Thus, in theory, affirming the bicultural voices of Black adolescents means to position youths so they are able to challenge the institutional narratives and media images that misrepresent them before the public. Bicultural affirmation, then, is predicated on pedagogical practices that emphasize the cultivation of academic skills in the classroom. The cultivation of such skills helps to reconcile, in part, the problems *and* promises of double consciousness by allowing Black youth to appropriate selectively dominant cultural tools as well as to develop resources that link young people to their cultural heritage. Rigorous curricula of this sort cultivate cultural negotiation response patterns within Black students that allow them to form ethical alliances across points of social differences and to participate fully in a culturally democratic and socially just society.

In a Different Room: Toward an African American Woman's Ethic of Care and Justice

Andrea D. Green

So I never knew that my skin was too Black
I never knew that my nose was too flat
I never knew that my clothes didn't fit
And I never knew there were things that I missed
And the beauty in everything
Was in her eyes.

> —Ysaye Maria Barnwell,
> "No Mirrors in My Nana's House"

A STUDY of stereotypes in the U.S. labor market has shown that racial stereotypes held by Whites raised barriers to job promotions and upward mobility in hiring practices. The main reason White respondents resisted hiring or promoting African American women was "the single mother thing" (Browne, 1999). The employers interviewed tended to "focus" on single motherhood as the "defining characteristic" of Black women, regardless of whether the women actually were single mothers who fit the common cultural stereotype of "matriarch" (Browne, 1999).

This is just one of the scripts Black women are read in the discourse on equal opportunity. It is as if a mirror image of Black women like me (and people who identify themselves as I do) were available for me to peruse while in a "different room." What I hear and what I see in these labels and scripts do not "fit" the person that I am. When some European Americans think of African Americans, Janie Ward has observed, "issues of moral behavior frequently spring to mind, for example, the escalating crime statistics (the immorality of delinquency and violent behavior) or teen pregnancy, single motherhood, and welfare recipiency (the immorality of sexual promiscuity and traditional family breakdown)." She goes on, however, to acknowledge that, while we know that "some of our behavior to others may seem self-contemptuous, when we turn our gaze inward, we have a different story to tell" (Ward, 1991, p. 268).

The epigraph at the beginning of this chapter, from "No Mirrors in My Nana's House" (Barnwell, 1992), captures the essence of the view from a different room. In the song, performed by members of the consciousness-raising singing group, Sweet Honey in the Rock, we discover that "No Mirrors" is a celebration of a woman knowing and understanding who she is. The cause for celebration lies in the security of knowing that "rightness," beauty, and the category of "person" is freely offered in the eyes of a loving grandmother and an elder in a community of people. In these lyrics we see that Whiteness can come in the form of a particularly foreign and harmful voice that tells the otherwise happy and secure African American woman that her skin is "too Black," her nose and feet are "too flat," and her clothes "don't fit" (Barnwell, 1992).

This essay privileges this different room of African American women, where the beauty of the self is not distorted by mirrored images that do not reflect who we are and where we are not confined to narrow descriptions of care and justice. The presence of "a different room" suggests a shift in location and point of reference. In addition, this allusion signifies entry into a contextual space, where we may begin to speak of knowledge and morality from the landscape and in the terms of Black women. The movement assumed is a shift in the locus of normative authority from that implied by modern philosophical liberalism toward the "truths" embedded in the indigenous spirituality of the African Diaspora.

To illuminate this room, I explore the limitations of objectivism and constructivism, since both of these form the foundation for current moral theory. After I examine the objectivist and the constructivist positions, I will introduce the different view that I believe best characterizes African American women's experiences, that of "womanist" theological ethics. *Womanist ethics*, in short, is the cultural framework for moral agency negotiations constructed by Black women who question how the social realities of race, class, and gender function within the situations in which Black women live. Womanist ethics provides us with information about the norms of a community of women whose lived experience is rarely factored into the dominant culture's assessment of moral theory. It is a normative stance of support for the validity of the "difference" in moral norms and priorities developed by women in response to perilous social conditions.

OBJECTIVISM VERSUS CONSTRUCTIVISM
FROM OBJECTIVE SELF TO SUBJECTIVITY

At the heart of moral development theory is a question that demands to be heard and answered in a judicious manner: Can humans, being human, ever hope to "capture" reality as it is in itself, or is the human being hopelessly enmeshed in a reality only apprehended by description?

Objectivists

On one side of the question is Western philosophy's most renowned possession—"objectivism." Also called *positivism*, objectivism reflects the notion that science describes to us how things truly are in and of themselves—that reason and measurement are the basis for all scientific inquiry, that a chair is a chair, and that truth is the result of measured, methodical, and rational processes. This approach dominates the natural sciences and, to a somewhat lesser extent, the social sciences. This absolutist stance has found a comfortable home in the moral development debate. In the Kohlbergian "justice"-oriented position, for instance, rational subjects deliberate and form consensus on the interpretation of reality. This rationalist "objective" position maintains that universal principles of truth, knowledge, beauty, and justice converge in external constructs, in an "out there" that persons rationally negotiate, reconstruct, and apprehend. The Kohlbergian stage sequences, for instance, assess the extent to which individuals obtain this absolute and invariant truth and determine how well, once apprehended, this universal and absolute truth is manipulated by the moral knower. Once such knowledge is apprehended, a moral knower's engagement with the abstract knowledge of "rightness" can be observed by a researcher and objectively measured, presumably with the results being unchanged by social or historical events or by the presence and circumstances of the researcher. For objectivists, power and ideology are not a part of objective reality, for neither power nor ideology alters the intrinsic nature of things.

But, of course, this approach has problems. Who is the judge? Which person is selected to assume the task of absolutely naming the norms and of designating what constitutes right behavior and moral goodness? Second, Kohlberg's method evokes questions regarding the location of the knower, the process of knowledge itself, and the determination of truth in the process of making theory. In Kohlberg's theory, the moral knower is singular, universal, and absolute. Moral reasoning theory argues that a moral person singularly considers what is right and then acts upon the moral choice, independently of the context, the historical framework, and the social condition.

Furthermore, this approach assumes in the negotiation of possibilities that the person making a moral decision has access to certain mainstream knowledge, that the social situation for development lacks any impediments to free choice, and that the understanding of truth is reflected universally in all knowers. In other words, the justice orientation appears to assume that all people are equally educated, are free, and are not constrained by oppression or historical circumstances.

Constructivism

On the opposing side of the question lies a more recent philosophical tradition known for its suspicion of objectivism and for its clearly articulated opposition to undisclosed and inevitable practices of power and ideology at work in the "objective" enterprise. This opposing side, known as *postmodernist*, is sometimes negatively considered relativistic and is most often identified as a form of social constructivism (Rorty, 1999).

Feminist historians and critics of objectivist science, most notably Donna Haraway (1991) and Sandra Harding (1987, 1998), have charged that the objectivist moral perspective was incomplete and biased and that it left out the experiences and perceptions of women. Calling for "feminist" empiricism to reflect a more inclusive feminist perspective, they sought a theory that (1) paid attention to the location of the researcher and subject, (2) defined knowledge and truth as produced in connection with other people, (3) was dependent on the perspective of the study subjects, and (4) was validated by the language the subject herself used to describe herself and her life story (Harding, 1987).

Holding to a position advanced impressively by the late philosopher of science Thomas Kuhn in *The Structure of Scientific Revolutions* (1962), the postmodernists challenge objectivism by revealing and arguing that, and demonstrating *how*, social or political positions shape the framework for subsequent scientific work (cf. Kuhn & Udell, 2001). Nel Noddings (1995) also notes that constructivism can be understood variously as "a philosophy, an epistemology, a cognitive position, or a pedagogical orientation"; the "basic premise is that all knowledge is constructed; knowledge is not the result of passive reception" (p. 115).

The constructivist, for instance, would unveil a not-so-flattering snapshot of social Darwinism to demonstrate how power plays enter the construction of scientific knowledge. Besides outlining the observable traits characteristic of human superiority, social Darwinists also delineated observable traits of "primitive" humanity. They described behaviors they observed, but did not understand, as "feeblemindedness, criminality, weakness, and pauperism." The theories they generated assigned the terms *moral degeneracy* and *intellectual inferiority* to people of difference, people who happened to be Black, and other peoples of color. For generations, page after page of observations by sociologists, anthropologists, and psychologists consistently assigned the adjective *primitive* to persons who were different from them. For generations, researchers and theorists failed to consider the political issues involved. They themselves represented the cultural belief and language systems that were "objectively determined" to be "superior."

This example of the tension in constructing knowledge provides an entrée for considering the challenge posed by difference in the construction of knowledge in general and to moral theory in particular. Differences, such as those of race, gender, or socioeconomic status, challenge moral theory because they raise concerns such as whether moral goodness is an external, fixed reality; whether an abstract and universal principle of moral reasoning exists that is intrinsic as a reference point in moral action; and whether the impetus for morality is formed as an expression of a relationship between individuals and their environments. Does the descriptor *moral goodness* depend upon the circumstances and the background—race, gender, social class—of the person asking the questions?

I believe that our constructions of knowledge need a methodological approach that considers the culture of the subjects who practice moral agency. The method should be one that does not inject, consciously or unconsciously, its social agenda into any subsequent theories. Thus, we are asking for a more democratic and egalitarian methodological practice. We also need a theoretical method that quells fears about relativism so that morality is not quashed by a flurry of simultaneously speaking voices that are incapable of being sensitive to distinct articulations, languages, cultures, and longings. However, to return to the metaphor of the mirror, we also need a theoretical approach to moral development that reflects an accurate image of women like me and not the image of an Other (Noddings, 1989). The method should recognize and respect, not simply include, people like me as long overdue members of the human project.

WOMANIST METHODS

A womanist theoretical orientation and methodology is an outgrowth of the ethic of care. Because the original justice/care debate framed difference largely in terms of male versus female orientations, the early ethic of care also participated in absolutist and essentialist linguistic practices. The early ethic of care included structural content that relied on descriptors of femininity and relationality. As the early ethic of care presented itself as another methodological orientation that tried to explain differences in the "self," exclusively on the basis of gender, it failed to be inclusive in a number of ways.

First, even though some might argue that the early ethic of care juxtaposes a woman's cultural ethos against Kohlberg's modern, objectivist ethic, it does not assist in our quest for a more democratic and egalitarian normative science. Even if the methodological shift from absolutism to constructivism is accomplished in *In a Different Voice*, the woman's ethos described therein is that of a mainstream White woman's social world and, thus, it cannot adequately capture the social reality of Black or other minority women. On a practical level, a convergence of structural factors allows (or forces, depending upon the position from which one views this) many Black women to live without men (Hurtado, 1996, p. 383). Because many Black women function within small predominantly female networks with fewer opportunities for female/male relationships, many different kinds of choices arise around potential relationships. Lynn Brown and Carol Gilligan (1992) found, and Garrett Duncan (chapter 2, this volume) also documents, that African American adolescent girls often "dis" (African American vernacular, short for *dis-miss, dis-regard*, or *dis-claim*) dominant constructions of femininity. From these examples, what appears more important than defining relationship or femininity for Black women is attending to the often competing claims of allegiance that impose the psychic pain of living out the conflicting roles of being both Black and woman.

The embodied and relational knower is revealed by a paradigm-shifting reliance on artistic forms to interpret voice and vision. Agency and identity are processed through narrative art rather than through normative science. Affect, emotion, and imagination form a three-dimensional reality. The narrative art of the subject provides and transcends the Kohlbergian "scoring," early Gilligan "coding," and later Gilligan "reading" of her own life story. A woman's moral narrative is "normed" against her earlier stories and those of other women who identify themselves as she does. This approach reflects feminist social science methodology, because it takes women's experience seriously and allows the subject to position herself through her choice of language, style, and behavior.

The switch from objectivist to feminist social science disorients the cultural preoccupation with a masculine viewpoint and creates space in the room for previously unheard people and voices. This aesthetic practice thus enables a postmodern project in democracy by deepening the benefits of freedom and justice beyond the formal structures that traditionally sink the democratic enterprise. In this case, the aesthetic art allows us free movement into a cultural ethos in which we hear Black women's voices on our own terms (Taylor et al., 1995). We have, in the paradigm shift from self to subjectivity and from absolutism to culturalism, entered into the different room of Black women's culture.

This "method" is itself one of womanism's key normative values; that is, it is a mandate to understand African American folk language because the moralisms in Black folk culture were remembered and transmitted in the language of the folk community in order for that community to remain independent of the dominant society. When African Americans hear the phrase *spoken word*, it may conjure images of hip-hop and rap music. Reference to the spoken word also may evoke the oral-aural performances characteristic of what is sometimes called "Black preaching." While both the speech forms of music and preaching are related, they share a common ancestry with a lesser known strand of speech performance found in West African traditions of the *griot*. The griot, the African social historian who performed his or her historical narratives to an urgent and demanding drumbeat, disappeared from African American culture when drumbeating was prohibited in the southern United States. African Americans quickly invented a substitute for the drum—speech delivered with the urgency of the drumbeat and uttered either by the narrator/musician or by the listeners in solidarity with the message. The power to speak became closely aligned with the power to heal in community. Folk language, expressed in many forms, still raises vital social issues to consciousness and is capable of calling people to be who they were created to be and can be. The failure to understand that morality can be an essentially spoken and dynamic process dims the possibility of grasping how profound are the truths bequeathed through the generations.

A womanist method is used by those predominately African American female scholars whose research reveals the norms and ideals of the African American community. These scholars gather and analyze narratives and connect those narratives to communal moral values. They construct the moral values by "connecting" what they receive from the knowing community (see Hekman, 1995, p. 19). These virtues must be understood as public virtues. Through the study of Black women's literature, poetry, and other art forms, womanist ethicists discover the "truths" for Black women held in the folk traditions of the African Diaspora.

WOMANIST VALUES

The moral values of womanism are the normative virtues and strategies that the African American woman inherited, retained, and developed despite the uncaring injustice inflicted on her race and sex, in order to save herself, her family, and her community (Walker, 1983; cf. Yancy, 2000). The task of moral development research from a womanist perspective must be to seek the normative discourses prevailing in communities of African American women. I will, therefore, explore the scholarship on and the lives of Black women for "archetypal" sociomoral representations of being Black and being woman that will make evident indigenous race-related knowledge that constitute norms for the moral enterprise. Such knowledge is held and practiced by many African Americans, knowledge that "grows out of and in turn informs" (Cannon, 1988, p. 290) the quality and availability of sociomoral relationships with all others in the human family. Real models of moral character, however, lie in the texts of Black cultural performances and oral narratives—folklore, spirituals, blues, work songs, fiction, autobiographies, poetry.

Cannon explores the literary tradition of Black women as a source for the values, norms, and priorities that are hidden in various myths, traditions, and rituals of women. Focusing on the work of Zora Neale Hurston, Katie Cannon (1995) has unearthed images of "Black-woman-subjectivities" shaped by a psyche actively resisting dominant hegemony and its products (e.g., resistance toward assimilation, unction, quiet virtue, folk language, interconnection). Paris (1995), by studying African spiritual survivals within African American religious and moral values, identified still other African American and pan-African virtues (e.g., beneficence, forbearance, practical wisdom, improvisation, forgiveness, and justice). Drawing from and building upon this prior research, I will discuss five of the values central to womanism. Although these themes are not absolutely unique to the African American community, they do form the foundation of the values at the core of womanism.

Improvisation

The ability to "think on one's feet," "make do," and "get by"—to improvise when other resources are unavailable—is a gift to individuals that benefits their communities (Paris, 1995). Becoming a morally informed knower requires doing and practice, so much so that the moral knower becomes transformed into a person whose moral knowing is intuitive—ethical values and actions are known to be valid through an immediate knowing. Where resources are limited and restricted, the lives of African American women present opportunities to creatively nuance well-understood moral precepts into different forms of moral action for different contexts. When moral knowing and art unite, the mixture reflects the moral knower's creativity and spontaneity, along with her spirit of perceptive wholeness. This can be shown through the stories of two women, each named Ella.

Ella Fitzgerald created a way out of no way when she thought on her feet and created the jazz forms known as *scat* and *riffs*. Oral tradition maintains that Ella forgot the words to a song she was performing before a large all-White audience. Knowing that her memory lapse would be associated with the supposed inferiority of all Black people and that she'd fail to "make Black folk proud," she moved and sang nonsense syllables with the musical score. The musical form delighted the audience and is still a vital form of expression in jazz. A musical icon and legend, Ella trusted her intuition and improvised a new way out of no way.

With a clear desire to see the energy of the Montgomery bus boycott ignite into a grassroots mass movement for civil rights, civil liberties, and social justice, Ella Baker accepted a call to create a southern U.S. office and a presence for the newly formed Southern Christian Leadership Conference (SCLC). Leaving her beloved New York for Atlanta in January 1958, Baker began SCLC activity from her room at the Savoy Hotel on Auburn Avenue. With very little money and no administrative support, she typed her own letters, prepared press releases, called all over the South from a pay telephone in the hotel hallway, and copied necessary documents on the mimeograph machine after hours at Ebenezer Baptist Church. Within 6 weeks of her arrival in Atlanta, Baker had not only started SCLC operations, but also mobilized voter registration efforts in cities and towns across the South into a focused, concentrated, well-executed force. Dubbed the Crusade for Citizenship, Baker's work coordinated teach-ins, registration drives, and voter rallies throughout the South. Even as an Associated Press news story suggested that Baker's Crusade work was "less than positive," Baker gave an accounting to Martin Luther King Jr. that local leaders from "New Orleans, Baton Rouge, Shreveport, Mobile, Tallahassee, Jacksonville, Nashville, Chattanooga, Knoxville, and Durham all had something to report" (Grant, 1998, p. 107). In the case of both these Ellas, the ability to move beyond limitations by utilizing whatever resources were available characterizes their actions. Their moral knowing was intuitive.

Unction

Cannon unearthed the term *unction* from African American folk culture to demonstrate the power of our tradition, just as Alice Walker retrieved the term *womanist* from the folk term *womanish*. Unction represents a sort of Black-woman mode of being that asserts the prerogative to "dis" (Cannon, 1988, 1995). In this cultural ethos, we can see, hear, and understand the cultural messages that teach Black women that "dis-ing" the metaphorical mirror is appropriate because it reflects distorted images of ourselves. Acting on cues, or conventions within Black culture, Black women come to equate the action of dis-ing the mirror with emotional health and strength. A Black woman can, and frequently does, opt to commit a "willful" counter-conventional act of naming her reality for herself and of defying the traditionally accepted race and gender niches of where others think she belongs. She can also move forward to identify others in the process of defying the barriers imposed at the intersection of race, gender, class, and sexual orientation. This denial of another's culturally constructed conception of who she ought to be is often expressed through acts perceived in the African American community to be outrageous, audacious, courageous, or willful behavior (i.e., Walker's definition of *womanist*). These behaviors represent a marked transition point.

Pauli Murray, raised in Durham, North Carolina, the granddaughter of a slave and the great-granddaughter of a slave owner, helped organize the first nonviolent sit-in demonstrations that successfully desegregated Washington, DC, restaurants in 1943. At the time she helped organize the demonstrations, she was the only female in her law school class at Howard University. Even though Murray subsequently became a feminist lawyer, teacher, poet, and Episcopal priest, her autobiography reveals that her greatest sociomoral growth occurred during a period of "bitter defeat," great personal setbacks, and a subsequent courageous act of womanist unction.

In 1938, years before the more easily recalled incidents at the Universities of Mississippi and Alabama, Murray applied for admission to the law school at the University of North Carolina (UNC), igniting a media frenzy and public debate over social justice and racial equality. Seven days after the date of her application, Murray's hometown (mainstream) newspaper, the *Durham Morning Herald*, headlined, NEGRESS APPLIES TO ENTER CAROLINA. Regarding Murray's application, North Carolina's governor told the state General Assembly, "North Carolina does not believe in social equality between the races and will not tolerate mixed schools for the races . . . but the White race cannot afford to do less than justice for the Negro" (Murray, 1987, p. 118).

Murray's challenge to UNC was well documented in the African American press, as the *Durham Carolina Times*, the *Baltimore Afro-American*, and the *Norfolk Journal and Guide* made Murray a household name. Where, in Murray's assessment, the southern White press deemed the identity of the "Negress" unimportant, the African American weekly papers, such as *The Crisis*, were anxious to give a name and a face to the woman who "submitted her application to the South" (Hutchinson, 1939, p. 105). The whirlwind about her was already overwhelming, but for Murray the comments of James E. Shepard, then president of the North Carolina College for Negroes (now North Carolina Central University), and a letter from her very dear "Aunt Pauline" shocked her into realizing the precarious nature of her social position. As Shepard pressed for the development of graduate programs at his own North Carolina College, he said of Murray's application, "Negroes could do their best work only in their best schools" (1987, p. 119). And from her aunt, Murray learned of the real fears her family held about their home being torched, about being fired from their jobs. She read, "You see you may hurt Dr. Shepard's cause for a (separate) university by beginning the fight . . . I think the state of N.C. wants this" (Murray, 1987, p. 119). Thus, Murray learned that her application to renegotiate the public education contract also redefined traditional racial and gender niches. After she had defied the traditional boundaries that race and gender placed upon her person, more clarity about the scope of her challenging act in 1938 was yet to come.

Following those tumultuous months, the dean of the graduate school of UNC determined that he could not grant Murray admission to the university, because "members of your race are not admitted to the University" (p. 115). Both a law school and a graduate school were developed at the North Carolina College, but Murray began to see the contours of a moral dilemma before her—"how not to oppose Negro universities per se while simultaneously exposing as unrealistic, and perhaps cynical, the state's attempt to set up separate graduate schools" (p. 124).

Murray's unction, her willful and courageous behavior, is revealed when she writes, "What I felt was the galling disappointment of personal defeat, and it was only later that I made a surprising discovery. . . . Every submission was accompanied by a nagging shame, which no amount of personal achievement in other areas could overcome. When I finally confronted my fear and took a concrete step to battle for social justice, the accumulated shame began to dissolve in a new sense of self-respect. For me, the real victory of that encounter was the liberation of my mind from years of enslavement" (p. 128).

Suspicion of Assimilation

Resistance to assimilating the narratives of White culture is a form of unction, but this resistance specifically hinges on the dangers inherent in appropriating the ways and perspectives of the mainstream. Any theory of Black women's moral development should first attend to a serious issue, namely, the social and collective process of selecting or rejecting dominant cultural values. It should include a serious engagement with the construction of cultural norms and the interactive processes that assure accountability between Black women and their communities of allegiance. Because what we know about how we see ourselves, and what we can know about how we become ourselves, is threatened by postmodern confusion and conveniently forgotten in the race for "progress," we are facing a moral dilemma in such a way that we cannot afford to completely miss the point or even to significantly misread it.

Like the adolescent voices described by Duncan in the previous chapter, Black women's voices express a worldview that questions the authority of the claims in absolutist, mainstream truth assumptions (Cannon, 1995, p. 60). This is not to say that the rejection of the mainstream truth claims is a cognitive process in which every Black woman is engaged. Rather, through a social process of selecting or rejecting dominant claims and values, Black women may choose to listen instead to the set of cultural cues from our mothers, our "Nanas," and the community of African American women at large. To give a personal example, I suspect that the "different room" is in danger of becoming lost to us in the labyrinth of everyday life. Many young Black women, participating in multiple cultural conversations, receive conflicting messages about who they are, whose they are, how they should live, and who they should be. Many women believe that the metaphorical mirror—the site of distorted scripts—that I have referenced herein provides them with a choice between United States–styled modern liberalism and African diasporism. But United States society is currently becoming a place where they may never discover and know how to uncover their own personal and communal "power" to construct healthy resistant scripts for themselves. If Africanist communal knowledge and womanist ethics are lost in the assimilative blender of Eurocentric individualism and materialistic class competitiveness, then the survival of the Black community will be "the" contemporary moral dilemma of Africans in America (cf. Cannon, 1988, 1995)

Interconnectedness

Interconnection constitutes the central ingredient of the conventions of care of self and others and is the basis for a dual public ethic of Black self-reliance and community support of the individual. Interconnection is an implied norm in the folk traditions and the language of the folk. Like the womanist research method itself, the determination of Black womanist ethics is hermeneutical: It connects women and girls (sometimes from different sociocultural perspectives) in the production of knowledge so that they can learn about each other.

Mary Belenky (Belenky, Bond, & Weinstock, 1997, pp. 267–269), while interviewing the Black women at the Center for Cultural and Community Development and reading Black literary works by Zora Neale Hurston, Alice Walker, and Toni Morrison, suddenly noticed herself witnessing an ongoing conversation in a different-culture "room." Aware of her own White ways of thinking, she knew she stood on the periphery as a witness to the shared drama of African American lives. Indeed, Belenky stood in a hazy transitional space, a social location marginal to her own epistemological senses, from which she could see through an open door into a room with African Americans at the cultural center. Belenky observed two practices that she judged to be of uncommon importance in African-based counterpublic spaces: art-making and experiential pedagogy (1997, p. 233). African American art and experiential learning are both collaborative and communal in the sense that they are public cultural processes. As one completes a form of art, one "knows" when the experiential form and the community from which it emerges is a match, and the project is shared with the larger community. As Brown and Gilligan (1992) note, we come to know and to know of others as subjects in relationships when "we listen for the plot (cultural and institutionalized restraints and conflicts) and for the voice of 'I' or self" (p. 28). Our cultural norms and values become part of our moral voices; our communities of allegiance shape, and are shaped by, our ought(s) and our right(s) and wrong(s) and ourselves. African American women find positive self-images in the webs of connection in which we live.

Spirituality

African American moral virtues are understood as, ultimately, divine gifts; these gifts, in turn, strengthen spiritual well-being and moral usefulness (cf. Spencer, Fegley, & Harpalani, 2003). To inherit the Divine gifts of the virtues, that is, requires the gifted person to share them with others. To practice African virtues is to participate in the knowledge, that is, in the oral-aural traditions, of the African Diaspora. African moral conventions involve a tradition of performed moral discourse, which involves rhyme, alliteration, sing-and-shout, and speaking the words in shamanistic fashion to the community in a cadence.

Similar to the mainstream ethos, the African ethos contains elements of male supremacy, and its values reflect "royal" or "princely" virtues with assumptions that men are natural leaders. Yet these precepts, though male biased, model the Ideal-Being-in-Community. Leaders stand accountable to the communities they represent or signify, but more awesome still is their accountability to the Supreme Deity (Paris, 1995, pp. 154–159). Similarly, African American role models (queens and kings), moral exemplars, and "wise folk" are so chosen for their healing and strengthening power to stand accountable to the community and to the community's God. The salient content of their moral substance lies in their ability to mediate social moral discourses with divine ethical imperatives and sponsor specific social-religious narratives that work best for the community.

Robert Coles's (1995) children's story about Ruby Bridges, the African American girl who integrated Frantz Elementary School in New Orleans in 1960 at the age of 6, provides an outsider's view of the strength of the African American oral-aural traditions. Coles suggests that the Bridges family's reliance upon prayer, a strong faith tradition, and sense of family equipped young Bridges with an almost incredible strength and resilience and an enormous capacity to forgive even people who do "bad things." Coles recalls how the young girl was once asked what she said to an angry, screaming mob of women and men. Bridges replied with irritation that she was not talking to the mob. "I was praying. I was praying for them. Please, God, try to forgive those people. Because even if they say those bad things, they don't know what they are doing" (Coles, 1995, p. 24; cf. Bridges, 1999; Coles, 1964).

Less explicit in Coles's account is how young Ruby Bridges, through the counsel of her family and church, understood herself to be a special actor in a God-driven drama to create a just, inclusive, and compassionate community where there had been none. Viewed from this Africentric perspective, we would see that young Ruby was divinely "chosen" to engage her life to protest values and norms that prohibit beloved community (cf. King, 1963c). Because Ruby accepted her call to perform in a justice-seeking spiritual drama, she became heir to divine gifts such as radical compassion, courage, sustained dignity, and the strength so necessary to fulfill her role.

Four decades later, Ruby Bridges (1999) writes that her life has not been without its share of adversity. Her hopes of going to college were dashed when she could not garner the necessary financial resources for school tuition. Her father died when she was 24; her brother died some years later in the early 1990s, leaving behind young children. Feeling somewhat defeated and searching for a "greater (life) purpose" (p. 57), Ruby determined that helping to parent her deceased brother's young children would facilitate her search for meaning. For her young nieces and nephews, Ruby again entered Frantz Elementary School, this time as a volunteer parent liaison and advocate. What Ruby discovered is a phenomenon typical of inner city schools. The once all-White and integration-resistant school was then struggling with an insufficient local tax base, leading to inadequate school funding for programming and de facto African American segregation.

Ruby Bridges (1999) found herself again resisting segregation while advocating equal opportunity. Asserting that "something bigger" than herself (p. 60) had chosen her for this work, Ruby set herself toward ensuring that all schools have adequate resources for all children. Starting with Frantz, she and the supporters who gathered about her were able to hire teachers for after school classes in areas such as ballet, African American dance, and manners and etiquette (p. 60). The publication of her life story, the Disney™ movie of the same, television and public appearances, book signing engagements, and various donations thrust Ruby into her current role as a leader in justice-seeking work. With the Ruby Bridges Foundation, funded by the proceeds of the picture book, *The Story of Ruby Bridges* (Coles, 1995), she works to ensure that the Frantz Elementary School and other similarly socially situated schools are "good enough to attract a healthy racial mix . . . [so] kids of different races grow up and live and work together in harmony"(p. 58).

Although she felt that "her life grew away" from her at times in the past, she now proudly asserts, "I know that experience comes to us for a purpose" (p. 61). As something of a validation, Ruby has received two honorary college degrees, demonstrating that the "folk" choose their leaders and moral exemplars for, and by, their God-given ability to heal and strengthen a broken world.

CONCLUSION: WOMANISM ENLIVENS THE SCRIPT
FOR FULLER PARTICIPATION IN LIFE

The ethics of womanism coalesce to build "a different room." In this "place," one's being and moral dignity are affirmed by the "folk" to counteract the disempowering messages of dominant culture. "Womanist-spaces," understood in the context of Gilligan and her colleagues' "webs of relationships," are profoundly informative because they provide thresholds for understanding the functions of the community. Thus, the theories of the embodied, relational knower and of womanist ethics have much to offer to a framework through which we can understand the conventions in Black women's moral reasoning. From both, Black women have opportunities for undistorted understandings of not only who we have been but also who we are.

What womanist ethics has taught us is that our foremothers coded African images of exemplary moral values into forms that remain hidden from dominant view. Consequently, we find these messages lurking in the background of "our" various cultural performances and social enactments—our words, our poetry, and our music. Creating, shaping, and sharing our stories through narrative and in art initiates a moral connectedness. In reality, the conventional virtues of improvisation, unction, suspicion of assimilation, interconnectedness, and spirituality are conveyed not in dominant mainstream stories, but in the cultural stories of the African American community. There is, in other words, a conversation in progress. The conversation proceeds across time and across space. The conversation is one of continued biological pro-creation, familial co-creation, and societal generativity against the odds.

Looking back over this survey of womanist virtues, we may realize that we have uncovered a way to speak of cultural or ethnic racial difference. Racial difference is not biologically or geographically determined, but it is determined by the context of our knowledge, the cultural framework that shapes us in our understanding of right and wrong. We have digressed from the modern notion that all human behavior conforms to a universal set of natural laws. We have envisioned a room where knowledge is constructed, perceived, and experienced differently in different cultural contexts.

Perhaps in this room, Black women and White women, Latinas and women from the Third World, and others who care to stand with us can understand moral agency in similar ways, where people from all types of "different room" communities can honor and appreciate our differences. This morality is a free space where the politics of recognition are freely lived and where successful coalition building and cross-cultural sociomoral relationships can occur. Perhaps this is an expression of a new "universal": people from many "different room" communities converging to negotiate who and whose they are in a common household of humanity, a house where they are free to roam, where they are welcomed by name and recognized as they wander from room to room. The immediacy of the whole range of human consciousness enriches the text of democratic possibility. Life cannot exist without difference because difference enlivens the script with richer and deeper possibilities for participating fully in the human project.

PART II

AFRICAN AMERICAN CONTRIBUTIONS TO PROMOTING MORAL FORMATION WITHIN SCHOOLS

WHEN ONE no longer assumes colorblindness—that African Americans are Anglo-Americans who simply wound up being born Black, one can no longer assume that "the Black child would profit by the close imitation of his White counterpart" (Wilson, 1978, p. 6). This suggests that promoting care, justice, and moral formation within schools requires that teachers be multicultural educators as well as moral educators.

MORAL EDUCATION AND RACE

Lawrence Kohlberg had a long-standing interest in reducing prejudice and in advancing civil rights through education. In a 1968 letter to the president of the University of Chicago, he strongly advocated that "sizable numbers" of African Americans "should be specially encouraged or supported to enter the University in disregard of the regular selection criterion" (1968b, p. 3). In 1975 he and Florence Davidson, his recently graduated doctoral student, co-authored a pioneering paper on "the cognitive-developmental approach to inter-ethnic attitudes" (Kohlberg & Davidson, 1975; cf. Davidson, 1974; Davidson & Davidson, 1994). Here they posited that higher levels of moral maturity were positively associated with racial tolerance. To support their claim, they briefly reported Davidson's (1974) study of "White, Negro, Jewish, and Oriental" children, which showed a decline in prejudice with increasing age. This they attributed to children's maturing sense of justice reasoning. The authors then speculated that prejudice could be reduced through moral education, particularly through Socratic discussion of moral dilemmas and the formation of an inter-ethnic Just Community School. Remarkably, Kohlberg was subsequently involved with the founding of five such Just Community Schools.

Yet Kohlberg was nearly deaf to different cultural voices and the necessity of multicultural education. Like an uninformed missionary who is more successful at spreading Western values than mature faith, he transplanted a model of moral education he had discovered in a high school in Israel to high school students in the United States. Most of the American students enrolled in his Just Community School interventions were from racial, social-class, and religious backgrounds that were different from those of Kohlberg and his original students. Nevertheless, few culturally sensitive changes were made to adapt the program to the backgrounds of the students participating in his interventions. Inevitably, his Just Community Schools were the least successful when the students were the most dissimilar to Kohlberg and the most successful when they reflected his background (Snarey, 1995).

OVERVIEW OF PART II: FROM CARE IN THE PAST TO MORE CARE-FULL SCHOOLS IN THE FUTURE

The three chapters in part 2 are a response, in part, to the inadequacies of homogeneous moral education in the classroom. Presenting African American perspectives on moral education, the authors of these chapters infuse multicultural sensitivity into Lawrence Kohlberg's concern with just school communities and Carol Gilligan's emphasis on the importance of a caring school atmosphere. They aim to provide an overview of questions of race in the education of African American students while holding in view the caring that fortified the segregated environments of African American schools. In addition, these authors describe the ways in which caring continues to be manifested, or, on a less positive note, point out that it is virtually absent in efforts to shape the education of African American students today.

This section begins with a synthesis of the research on segregated schools by Vanessa Siddle Walker and Renarta Tompkins in chapter 4. Their essay provides an overview of the ways that African American educators cared, personally and institutionally, for the children they served. Siddle Walker and Tompkins propose that such caring in African American segregated schools concerned itself with the whole child and that the interpersonal and institutional forms of caring reinforced one another. The authors also reason that this level of caring was a means through which African Americans sought to achieve a just society, and vice versa. Overall, these historic schools embodied both institutional caring and justice by identifying the needs of students and by deliberately creating and maintaining structures to meet those needs. Care and justice thus worked in conjunction and inseparably in the world of segregated schools. Moreover, an understanding of these educational communities supplies an important context for raising questions about the lack of success experienced by many African American children in schools today.

Moving from the past to the present, Edward P. St. John and Joseph Cadray in chapter 5 ask of desegregation, "Is it just and caring?" Using a case study in which members of a teacher education faculty examine their own beliefs about diversity, St. John and Cadray demonstrate that, without intervention, desegregated schools cannot fulfill the dreams of integration. Conversely, intervention may cause teacher educators to alter their educational strategies to help create desegregated schools that will maintain the caring that existed in previously all-Black segregated schools. The authors conclude by arguing that practical discourse among educators must go beyond the justice and legal standards for desegregation to include a commitment to care. Their thoughtful demonstration of the implementation of justice, without attention to caring, is a sobering description of what happens when one facet is attended to without commitment to maintaining the other.

With a surprise ending, Jennifer Obidah and her colleagues, Marquita Jackson-Minot, Carla Monroe, and Brian Williams, provide a final challenge in chapter 6. How will teachers steeped in an African American teaching tradition negotiate school environments that focus primarily on "crime and punishment"? What kinds of dilemmas are created for both teachers and students? Using a moral dilemma that erupted in an inner-city classroom, these researchers explore what happens when the moral understandings of students and school officials are contradictory. In particular, they discuss the role of teachers who live on the precipice where upholding inflexible school rules for the general good may mean harming specific students who already live and learn in precarious circumstances. The essay vividly reminds us that, even when universities produce teachers with an awareness of the cultural tradition of African American teaching, schools must create institutional structures that will not undermine attempts to care. To seek just ways of handling community violence and protecting students, without concurrently expressing care for the individual student, pits justice and care as oppositional rather than collaborative.

Together, these three essays provide a series of important issues about the role of care and justice, especially when African American education is viewed over time. We begin with a look back to the schooling that African Americans experienced in the South before desegregation.

CHAPTER 4

Caring in the Past: The Case of a Southern Segregated African American School

Vanessa Siddle Walker and Renarta H. Tompkins

> As an American Negro, I consider the most fortunate thing in my whole life to be the fact that through childhood I was reared free from undue fear of or esteem for White people as a race; otherwise, the deeper implications of American race prejudice might have become a part of my subconscious as well as of my conscious self.
> —James Weldon Johnson, *Along This Way*

TWO LITERATURES have emerged concurrently over the past 3 decades—independent of each other in disciplinary base and yet inextricably linked in orientation. One literature casts a new look at the segregated schooling of African Americans. Accepting the belief that the schools were inferior in equality of resources and distribution of school funding, contributors to this literature sought to look beyond justice issues, such as access and resource inequality, and explore the type of caring schools that African American teachers and principals had created within their segregated worlds (for review, see Siddle Walker, 2000). It brought to the forefront the voices of African American educators who were widely dismissed and ignored in the wake of desegregation efforts (Cecelski, 1994; Foster, 1997) and used these voices and archival data to reconstruct a history of African American schooling that looked beyond the inequalities to document what schools were able to create in spite of the inequalities. Much of this research clustered in the late 1970s and early 1980s, then re-emerged in 1991 and continues into the present.

To be sure, southern segregated schools for African Americans developed within an intentional system of neglect and opposition (Ashmore, 1954; Kluger, 1977). None of this research justifies or minimizes the inequalities; however, they do provide a different lens through which to view the schooling during the era. In book-length descriptions (Cecelski, 1994; Foster, 1997; Jones, 1981; Morris & Morris, 2000; Noblit & Dempsey, 1996; Siddle Walker, 1996), journal articles (Beauboeuf-Lafontant, 1999; Dempsey & Noblit, 1993; Foster, 1990, 1991; Irvine & Irvine, 1983; Jeffries, 1994; McCullough-Garrett, 1993; Siddle Walker, 1993a, 1993b; Sowell, 1974), and self-published histories (Davis, 1996; Edwards, Royster, & Bates, 1979; Tilford-Weathers, 1996), four characteristics have been documented that primarily explain the operation of the schools. These characteristics include (1) the presence of well-trained, professional teachers who were committed to providing educational opportunities for the children; (2) an extracurricular program that reinforced the belief that African Americans could be successful in a variety of arenas; (3) the parental support the schools received; and (4) the visionary leadership of the school principals. Embedded in each of these characteristics is the belief that caring was the very foundation of the education that occurred within segregated African American schools.

In a similar period, the studies on caring that are familiar to developmental psychologists, moral educators, and philosophers also entered public debate. In the years since Carol Gilligan eschewed the belief that justice best described the relationship of one human to another and to his or her life circumstances, moral care theory joined moral justice development theory as a theoretical system that specifically addressed schooling. For example, Jane Roland Martin (1992) and Nel Noddings (1992) expanded the reasoning to include a belief that schools should reflect the family-oriented, homelike environment embodied in the caring literature. Noddings (1992) concluded that caring was central to successful schooling because students work harder for teachers whom they like and trust; her premise has been verified in the findings of other researchers (Burke & Nieremberg, 1998; Peart & Campbell, 1999). Today, researchers continue to advocate caring as central in school development.

Ironically, however, the shared periods of growth notwithstanding, the literature on segregated African American schooling and the literature on caring schools have seldom been adequately informed by each other. With the exception of Noddings (1999), Noblit and Dempsey (1996), and chapter 5 by St. John and Cadray in this volume, all of which explore some aspect of school desegregation and caring, the fields stand strikingly removed and uninformed by the scholarship of each other. The result is an ahistorical stance on the part of moral educators that fails to incorporate the caring that existed in African American segregated schools, and an atheoretical perspective on the part of historians of segregated schools who seldom relate the caring they describe to prevailing theories of care and justice.

In this chapter we seek to inform the developmental and moral literature on caring and justice by providing an overview of the ways in which care and justice were constructed in the history of African American schooling. Specifically, we will (1) summarize the collective research on segregated schools to provide a thematic overview of the presence of caring and fairness within the schools, considering both interpersonal and institutional forms; and (2) discuss the ways in which these themes expand the theoretical literature on the ethical voices of care and justice. Principally, we will argue that a consistent message of care and a general agreement on what it meant to care were the constructs that allowed African American schools to buffer the injustices of inequality and prepare the students to live in and challenge a world of injustice. Thus, in the segregated educational world, caring and justice were not oppositional activities, but rather caring functioned deliberately and collaboratively to achieve justice. An understanding of this historical model of care expands current debates about caring and provides critical data for efforts to implement caring schools for African American children.

HOW TEACHERS AND PRINCIPALS PROVIDED PERSONAL CARE AND INTERPERSONAL FAIRNESS

The kind of relational caring that Noddings describes (here called *interpersonal* caring) permeated the environment of the segregated school. Interpersonal caring defines a state in which the person who is caring is concerned about, and willing to attempt to meet, the physical, psychological, and academic needs of the individual for that person is caring. Noddings (1992) notes that this kind of caring puts a good deal of responsibility on the teacher to be the caregiver most of the time. It also requires a knowledge of the student, since, as Noddings (1992) maintains, "we respond most effectively as carers when we understand the other's needs and the history of this need" (p. 23).

In segregated African American schools, both teachers and principals fulfilled the role of caregiver. Because limited professional ave-
nues were open to African Americans, these educators represented the
best and the brightest of the race (Altenbaugh, 1992; Foster, 1990) and
were increasingly well trained in their professional knowledge (Siddle
Walker, 2000). They also generally came from the community in which
they taught or from similar African American communities. As a result, the teachers brought to the classroom a good deal of understanding about the needs of the students and, with the assistance of their
professional organizations, could use this knowledge to enhance their
understanding of particular student needs. Additionally, during this
period the African American community highly valued its schools as
a means by which to improve the educational, social, political, and economic circumstances of all African Americans; therefore, they willingly
vested teachers and principals with the intellectual and moral authority
to oversee the development of the race (Altenbaugh, 1992).

Within this context, teachers often played a variety of roles that
can be characterized under the attribute of care. While it is difficult
to separate the terms *care, nurture,* and *concern* in the literature because the teachers used them interchangeably, a synthesis of the
forms of caring in the segregated schools suggests four interrelated
forms of caring. Teachers evidence caring in their roles as counselors,
benefactors, encouragers, and race cheerleaders. These roles proved
similar across a variety of studies.

Counselor

In their 1954 Southern Association report, the teachers of Caswell
County Training School reported that their relationships with students were exceptionally good (Siddle Walker, 1996). At the root of
these relationships appear to be the roles they assumed as counselors.
Teachers made themselves available before school, during planning
periods, and after school to talk with students. Across the literature,
researchers report that teachers were open to students, understanding
of their problems, and willing to take the time to communicate with
them (Foster, 1997; Jones, 1981; Noblit & Dempsey, 1996; Siddle
Walker, 1996). Students reportedly felt comfortable talking to teachers
about personal problems as well as academic ones. For example, a student from Trenholm High describes her experiences with one teacher:
"I could talk to her like my mother" (Morris & Morris, 2000). While
teachers apparently did not violate students' confidentiality, and thus
demonstrated some degree of substantive justice, they did not abide by

Noddings's (1992) rule of being nonjudgmental and freely gave advice (Morris & Morris, 2000). Neither did they adhere to the other justice norms of respect for freedom and autonomy. Rather, teachers believed that they held a knowledge base that students did not have, and they dispensed advice in ways that they believed facilitated the growth of the individual and the race (see chapter 1).

The teachers also did not limit themselves to one-on-one counseling, but also sometimes used the classroom as a counseling forum. When a teacher believed that a particular discussion was in the best interest of the students, the teacher would put aside the curriculum to serve as counselor for the whole class. In Michele Foster's book, *Black Teachers on Teaching* (1997), Mr. Dawson speaks of his experience teaching in a segregated school:

> The biggest difference is that we were able to do more with the Black student in the Black school . . . if I wanted to come in this morning and have my children put their books under their desks . . . and ask why are you here? Are you here just to make another day? . . . Do you know where your competition is? Your competition is not your little cousin sitting over there. Your competition is that little White kid sitting over in the other school. He's the one you got to compete with for a job. (p. 6)

Mr. Dawson's speech to his students is an example of the most frequently cited illustations of care in segregated African American schools. This is the teacher whom students describe as "telling it like it is."

The counseling role also extended to the principal. The description of N. L. Dillard at Caswell County Training School provides a typical example (Siddle Walker, 1996). Students reportedly approached the principal with any problems they had, just as they would with their teachers. One teacher recalls: "I remember kids would come up and tell the secretary, 'I'd like to see Mr. Dillard.' And she would say, 'Let me see if he's busy,' and the [student would be allowed to go in.] He could talk to the students about pretty much anything" (p. 129). Likewise, a student remembers how easy it was to see the principal: "You did not have to worry your teacher to see the principal because you would see him sometime during the day. He took the time to talk to you. You did not have to set up appointments" (p. 129). Another student sums up the perception of many of his contemporaries: "He was never too busy to talk with you about your problems. Not only was he interested in you in school, he was interested when you left school. He knew all the children by name" (p. 129). Similar caring relationships between students, teachers, and principals were described in other research on segregated schools: Principals formed relationships with students, encouraged their success, admonished them when they had not met expectations, and provided opportunities for them to continue their education (Rodgers, 1976). As discussed below, however, they had their own forum for group counseling.

Encourager

A role closely related to that of providing advice or counseling students was that of encouraging students to move beyond what was expected of them and urging them to take on new challenges. Teachers in such roles assessed students' strengths and pressed them to be even better. A student spoke of one teacher, Mrs. Thomas, this way:

> She encouraged me to do a lot of other things. You know, read things that weren't just regular reading. . . . And, you know, to do things like the spelling bee. . . . That was Mrs. Thomas pushing me to do that. . . . She worked very hard with me on just whatever. But mostly it was encouraging me to do things. (Morris & Morris, 2000, p. 53)

In this case, the student felt that the teacher cared because she pushed her to do things she would not have done otherwise.

Encouragement also went beyond academic matters. Teachers demonstrated an interest in helping students behave appropriately in school settings. Another student explained his relationship with Mrs. Hyler:

> Mrs. Hyler was particularly tough on me. . . . But I never felt like it was negative. . . . I felt like that was her way of caring about us. . . . You know, I guess things were also a little physical in those days. Whenever I'd misbehave, she'd walk up behind me and hit me on the head, not hard but enough to get my attention. . . . I always remember when it happened, I chuckled, didn't laugh out loud. But it always made me smile because I knew I was being dealt with. (Morris & Morris, 2000, p. 54)

Mrs. Hyler's method of "dealing with" the student reflected the community values of the era. Her actions were the same that might be taken by a grandmother or aunt in prompting a student to "straighten out" his or her ways. Clearly, the recipient felt affection, not abuse, from this action. In some other settings, as well, a child could be disciplined for not learning the lesson or having not completed work (Davis, 1996; Foster, 1997).

Benefactor

A third role that demonstrated care was that of the benefactor. *Benefactor* is the term used to identify teachers and principals who helped students and their families personally by using their influence or resources. In many African American segregated schools, teachers and principals provided financial assistance for students to attend college and helped secure jobs for students not attending college. They also helped students and families in times of death or personal need and supplied transportation and resources when they assisted a child with educational needs (Siddle Walker, 2000). Littlefield (1999) found that teachers served this function by collecting food and clothes for needy students. These examples of caring are embedded in African American community values of helping (Noblit & Dempsey, 1996) and of distributive justice in that they reflect the community's concern that all members have equal claims to receive material and social benefits, regardless of income status (Kohlberg, 1984, pp. 621, 635; Raphael, 2001). Thus, teachers—as extensions of the community—embodied the values spectrum of the Black community and incorporated them into their own definitions of what it meant to care for students.

Teachers who acted as benefactors, in some cases, offered further provision in the larger community. For example, some teachers taught children during the day and parents in the evenings. These evening study programs were sanctuaries for illiterate people who wished to learn how to read and write; teachers received no additional compensation for this activity (Littlefield, 1999). Similar courses, especially after World War II, have been described in other settings (Siddle Walker, 1996).

Racial Cheerleader

A final essential role played by caring teachers and principals in the segregated school was that of racial cheerleader. Although this cheerleading could also occur in counseling or encouraging roles, the distinction here is with teachers who went beyond the curriculum to instill students with pride in their race and to make certain they understood their history and heritage. Madge Scott (Foster, 1997) provides a good example of racial cheerleading in many schools:

> Even though the schools were segregated, the teachers did quite a few things in the curriculum that did not coincide with the White school and were not sanctioned by the school board. The teacher taught us a lot

about our own race even though the school board prescribed a curriculum that didn't include anything much about Black people. (p. 38)

Some others describe these efforts as teaching more than what was required (Edwards et al., 1979). Others provide explicit information about how the teacher supplemented the curriculum with information about race and the African American presence in the United States (Noblit & Dempsey, 1996).

In sum, teachers variously assumed the roles of counselor, encourager, benefactor, and race cheerleader in dynamic response to student needs. Rather than neatly fitting into fixed roles, teachers embodied these qualities simultaneously and consistently over their careers. For African American teachers, caring was an integral part of being able to teach African American students effectively, a sentiment best captured by Ruby Forsythe: "It is impossible to discipline or teach Black children unless the children believe you care about them" (Foster, 1997, p. 31).

In many ways, the commitment the teachers held to teaching the children is embedded in the culture of the era. As Hundley (1965) describes it, the teachers were self-made. They were in "sympathy with the youth whose problems and aspirations they understood only too well" (p. 13). Usually products of southern segregated schools themselves, these teachers both intuitively identified with student needs and aspirations and, simultaneously, understood how to negotiate the world beyond the local community. Having lived out the benefit of education, they could also tell students how to move beyond the limited life possibilities of a segregated world and how to use education to achieve a middle-class life. In espousing the philosophies they held, they both re-created themselves in their students and made possible the continued advancement of a people with whom they were identified (Irvine & Irvine, 1983). Their point of identification with the children is captured vividly in Sowell's (1976) description of a principal who noted, "You are pushing for them, and dying inside for them, [but] you have to let them know that they have to produce" (p. 36).

In this intimate venue, students reportedly responded to their examples and descriptions of success. Their teachers were said to be "inspiring." Students didn't want to let them down. Consistently, they attributed their success and self-confidence to the work of their teachers. Quipped one student in Rougemont, North Carolina, "Preachers were good, but teachers were great!" (Noblit & Dempsey, 1996, p. 129).

HOW INSTITUTIONAL STRUCTURES REINFORCED
CARE AND JUSTICE

In addition to engaging in the same type of caring interpersonal interactions as did their own teachers, the principals and teachers engaged
in modes of institutional caring. By this we mean that they provided
the leadership for school structures that collectively communicated
to students their importance in the school community and provided
the students opportunities to develop in areas of need. The institutional structures most frequently identified in the segregated school
literature include four essential structures: the extracurricular activity
program, the assembly program, and the curriculum, and the homeroom plan.

Extracurricular Program

The principals and teachers at segregated African American schools
created types of activity programs for their students that were similar
to those of the schools of their more privileged counterparts. The limited funding made the implementation of these club activities more
difficult than that faced by White principals; nonetheless, every African American segregated school reported in the scholarly literature
had some array of clubs that were maintained by the principal and
teachers and financed, in part, by the African American school community. That the community supplied the funding assured a remarkable degree of distributive justice in that all students had opportunities to participate, not simply those students with more family
resources. Across the schools, these clubs included those focusing on
(1) musical ability such as in the glee club, the rhythm band, the cho-
ral club, band, dance, orchestra; (2) literary abilities, such as the Better
English Club, Drama Club, and newspaper; (3) vocational interests,
such as in the New Homemakers of America and Future Teachers of
America; (4) scholastic achievement, such as in the Crown and Scep-
ter Club and Beta Club; (5) moral development, such as in Hi-Y and
Just Us Club; (6) academic content extension, such as in La Circle
Française; and (7) personal interests, such as in the Library Club, Avia-
tion Club, and Pep Club (Rodgers, 1976; Siddle Walker, 2000).

Although the similarity of these activities with those of White
schools may suggest that the clubs were simply part of the educational landscape of the era, the specific purposes that principals articulate for the existence of the clubs in their schools give them primacy
in the educational context of African American children. In particular,

African American educators in segregated schools noted that African American children needed opportunities to develop their interests and talents because the segregated society in which they lived limited enrichment opportunities. Principals described the clubs as offering opportunities for students to learn to appreciate certain cultural activities, such as those in the performing arts, and opportunities to counter the negative influences and social inequalities outside the school hall. N. L. Dillard of Caswell County Training School in North Carolina, for example, noted his concerns about the lack of theater and other cultural arts and the fact that the pool hall provided one of the few forms of entertainment. Evidenced in teachers' and principals' commitment to opportunity and enhancement was the motivating desire for rectifying justice (cf. Kohlberg, 1984, pp. 622, 635; Raphael, 2001). Their motivation, that is, was drawn from their witnessing African American children's harsh treatment in the society to which they were bound, and they were confident that education could be an instrument to correct injustice and counteract inequality.

Reportedly, large numbers of students participated in the extracurricular program, often because teachers—in their benefactor role—used personal resources to be certain that students had transportation home or to other club-related events when necessary. Jones (1981) reported that the average number of extracurricular activities per student was three, with a range from one to nine. Dillard's (1942) survey of five high schools reported that each school had an average of 42 activities, with a range from 39 to 51, and that approximately one office existed for every three students to hold, with most students holding only one office. This distribution of activities and offices across the majority of the student body was important because it gave many students an opportunity for development. As Alice Withers indicated, "If you wanted to be a leader, there was something for you" (Siddle Walker, 1996, p. 107).

The extracurricular program illustrates both institutional caring and justice by identifying the needs of students and by deliberately maintaining structures to meet those needs. In particular, by insisting that the resources be generated by members of the African American school—rather than expecting individual students to assume the expense for particular activities—the principal and teachers could channel students into areas that best reflected talent and skills, rather than their parents' financial capacity. Admittedly, the program was implemented in the hands of caring teachers and principals; yet the structures stood above particular individuals and represented the philosophy and activities of the school. Indeed, this structure continued to meet the needs of students over time, with similar African American concepts of care and justice articulated for their existence, despite the departure of particular principals or teachers.

Assembly Program

The school assembly program, also sustained by a community ethos, similarly responded to children's needs. According to African American segregated-school research, students needed the opportunity to be exposed to ideas, to learn to behave in a cultural setting, and to perform (Siddle Walker, 1996; Hundley, 1965). Across the South, African American principals used this weekly forum to meet those needs. Typically, each club was assigned an assembly for the presentation of its activities. Sometimes major speakers were brought to lecture to the students; on occasion, local community people participated in events. Hundley (1965) wrote that because the students were "barred from theaters . . . and were seldom exposed to those stimulating discussions with people of other backgrounds that lift the spirit and develop the self-confidence" (p. 14), school assemblies served to fill this void.

The principals also generally played a central role in the assembly. Their "remarks" at the end or beginning of the program functioned as a collective expression of values and expectations. These talks appear to have emphasized some of the values the school community believed were important for students to hold. Davis (1996) describes these values as "self-improvement, discipline, responsibility, leadership, respect for authority, and thriftiness" (p. 32). Indeed, the talks were an example of the principal's functioning as a group counselor, encourager, and cheerleader.

A concrete example is demonstrated in the chapel talks given by N. L. Dillard. According to a former teacher, Mr. Dillard placed a significant value in these assemblies on African American children becoming educated:

> He used to say, "In this world today, the world you are going out in, you are going to have to be good, and extra good. You're going to have to be better. I don't care how many degrees you can go out and get, you are going to have to be better than that white man." He used to preach that (Siddle Walker, 1996, p. 110)

Across the schools, the principals' admonishments were grounded in a Christian ideology, embraced democratic values, and included references to the needs of African Americans.

This dual focus of the assembly—which simultaneously emphasized student talent and exposed them, in a group setting—to new ideas, fulfilled both the purposes of encouraging and educating. Like the clubs, these assemblies were institutionalized solutions for meeting the students' needs.

Curriculum

The segregated-school curriculum supported the private messages and classroom messages of teachers and principals who reinforced the aspirations of students to grow up and "be somebody." Through the term *being somebody*, the teachers and principals suggested that students were not to feel bound by the segregated world in which they lived, but were to believe that if they worked hard enough, they could "be anything they wanted to be." As such, the staff prepared the students to be participants in a nonsegregated world, even though this world did not yet exist in the South. In the curriculum, institutionalized caring was present in the expanded focus of the curriculum, designed to meet the needs and fuel the aspirations of African American children.

Academically, the schools that were surveyed sought whenever possible to be certain that the same curriculum was being offered to African American boys and girls as was being offered to White boys and girls. This belief was grounded in the general opinion among the educators that to succeed, the students had to be "better" than the students at the White schools. To offer a curriculum any less comprehensive than that offered at the White schools was to fail to give the students the tools they needed to succeed. Indeed, in many African American schools the principal and teachers sought to have more courses in their school than were available at the White school, an effort that was frequently undermined by White school board authorities who forced schools to stop such courses (Edwards, Royster, & Bates, 1979; Foster, 1997; Sowell, 1974, 1976; Siddle Walker, 1996). However, this effort was consistent with their belief that the African American child should know more in order to succeed. Likewise, their failure to engage in an either/or debate about classical academic training versus vocational training reveals their belief that students should have an array of learning opportunities available to them. Unabashedly, they offered both vocational and classical training, often requiring students to take both (Cecelski, 1994; Edwards, 1998; Jones, 1981; Siddle Walker, 1996).

The implementation of the curriculum is also noteworthy. Although the written curriculum paralleled that of the White schools, the curriculum as it was delivered reportedly often provided information to students on the roles that African Americans had played in science, literature, music, and other realms. As did the individual in-class expansions of curriculum discussed earlier, institutionalized schoolwide events reinforced the relationship of African Americans to the written curriculum. For example, many segregated schools observed Negro History Week and Emancipation Day. Reporting on Rougemont in Durham, North Carolina, Noblit (1993) notes that students were taught pride in being African American as they formed an understanding of "where we've been and what we need to do" (p. 129).

Of course, the curriculum in the segregated school was always constrained by financial needs, school size, and school boards. Nonetheless, the deliberate attention to curriculum, particularly the desire to implement a curriculum that would specifically address the needs of the students, is another example of how the institution creatively sought to encounter and offer an answer to the needs of students.

Homeroom Plan

Beyond the extracurricular activities, the assemblies, and the curriculum, some schools also provided other examples of institutional caring. One of these was the homeroom teaching plan, in which four or more teachers were assigned to act as homeroom teachers for an entering class of ninth-grade students. Each year, the teachers moved up to the following grade with the students, assuming all responsibilities for class needs, such as junior-senior prom, senior yearbook, and fund-raising activities. After having served as senior-class advisors, the teachers were reassigned to an incoming freshmen class and the process began again.

The homeroom plan was an important mechanism for facilitating relationships between teachers and students and for continuing to individualize admonishments about the school's expectations for their success. One teacher at Caswell County Training School talked about how in "following" a class for 4 years, "You get to know the student well. You had to accept them and love them." A student emphasizes that these "groups of teachers had a lot of concern and care and looked out after us for those four years. It became like a family" (Siddle Walker, 1996, p. 125).

The extensiveness of this program, however, is undocumented. Likewise, although some references occur in the literature to principals being unwilling to track students because of concerns about low expectations (Siddle Walker, 1996), extensive knowledge of this practice remains to be explored. However, the efforts that have been docu-

mented indicate that the African American school used institutionalized structures to meet the needs of African American children within
the context of a segregated society.

CONCLUSION: SEGREGATED AFRICAN AMERICAN SCHOOLS EXPAND CURRENT PARADIGMS

This overview of interpersonal and institutional caring within segregated African American schools highlights several significant dimensions of caring that should become part of contemporary discussions
of caring. First, examples of teacher and principal caring for individual
students interpersonally were supported by institutional structures
that sent similar messages to students. Thus, interpersonal caring was
supported by institutional caring. Caring did not exist in a vacuum,
but was modeled and implemented at every level of schooling.

Second, in addition to being delivered in a seamless way, the caring in the segregated-school environment appears not to have frag-
mented the child by addressing only one aspect of his or her developmental needs. For example, teachers did not confine themselves
simply to being concerned about the student's success in their particular subject. Rather, the nature of caring in the environment seems to
have been illustrated by the teachers expressing concern for the child's
academic development, his or her personal life, his or her future plans,
and so forth. Caring thus was not focused on one area of the child's
life only, but was a type of caring in which the one who cared was
willing to explore the plethora of concerns that could affect the child's
performance.

Third, caring was truthful. In contrast to a contemporary setting
in which Pajares and Graham (1997) describe teachers as being unwilling to give "true" feedback, teachers and principals were willing to be
truthful with students as part of their caring, both in their assessment
of individual performances and in their expectations for the group.
"You can't be just as good; you have to be twice as good." This statement, frequently made by teachers and principals, represents their belief about the realities of being African American in a segregated society: that the students could not be expected to be placed on equal
footing with their White contemporaries was not withheld from them.
Instead, the truth of this reality was consistently reinforced, even as
teachers attempted to inspire students to be challenged to overcome
the inequalities they faced. Many times, teachers and principals were
brutally honest in these instances of "colortalk" (see chapter 1).

Fourth, caring had a purpose. Both forms of caring were not offered simply as means to an end. Rather, caring was a form of commitment to justice. To care intensely for the students for whom they had been given responsibility was to provide them with a storehouse of tools for challenging and thwarting a deeply imbedded system of inequality. The teachers were very clear that they expected the students to help achieve justice for all the African Americans still struggling under oppression. This end could be accomplished when each child was educated to his or her highest potential. Caring was one means of educating them; thus, caring facilitated the end of justice. In this construct, caring and justice were not oppositional constructs but worked in deliberate, collaborative ways.

Finally, caring was not gender bound during this era. Students report that both male and female teachers cared for their needs and that both showed concern for fairness. Because of a history of oppression, African American women have historically been co-partners with men. Unlike White women of the era, African American women were encouraged to go to school. A school hierarchy based on gender did exist, with school principals, like preachers, typically being male. Nevertheless, women teachers were more accepted by men for their expertise—even in cases in which men were the leaders in the schools. In this context, caring appears to have been offered to both boys and girls by both male and female teachers. The common bond between women and the common bond between men was not superior to the common bond based on race, perhaps because segregated society did not allow African Americans to forget for one minute that they were defined by race.

This history of segregated schooling among African Americans in the South provides an important template on which to analyze the current experiences of African Americans in schools. Consider one example. The seamless delivery of messages of caring to African American children that occurred historically raises powerful questions in contemporary discussions about the role of a strong caring teacher who rallies his or her relational prowess to foster student development, while the larger institutional message seems to be the antithesis of care. For example, the ongoing higher percentages of African Americans being tracked into nonacademic curricula and of receiving suspensions and the lower percentages of African American children in academic clubs all send powerful institutional messages about the place of African American children within the school (Irvine, 1990). Arguably, these messages can undermine the efforts of individual teachers to motivate children to believe in what they are capable of achieving. Unless the larger institutional structures are corrected to facilitate a message of caring consistent with the interpersonal messages of caring, neither children nor their parents are likely to believe that African American children are being cared for. This failure may explain the distrust that many minority parents feel toward schools. Further, in schools where children lack care and affirmation, there is less motivation to apply oneself.

Educators and community leaders must begin to visualize ways to reconstruct the caring messages previously delivered to African American children. McAllister (1997) provides an example of a model after-school setting, and Ladson-Billings (1994) provides an example of how individual teachers have accomplished this in contemporary school settings. In both works, we see that the caring that has been central in African American history can be utilized to enrich the education of all children.

Justice and Care in Postdesegregation Urban Schools: Rethinking the Role of Teacher Education Programs

Edward P. St. John and Joseph P. Cadray

> Black kids need teachers who can understand and appreciate some-
> thing about Black communities. Too many White teachers don't under-
> stand Blacks and don't want to understand us, yet they expect us to be
> able to understand them.
>
> —Bernadine Morris, *Black Teachers on Teaching*

SOCIAL REFORMERS aimed to integrate schools through the desegregation of racially isolated educational systems. They had a
dream of African Americans, European Americans, and children of
other races learning together in just environments that promoted racial harmony (e.g., King, 1986). Reality, however, has proven to be
much different from the original dream (Morris, 1997). After nearly a
half century of court-mandated desegregation, a larger percentage of
African American children attend predominantly Black public schools
than before the Supreme Court's *Brown* decision in 1954, and among
the desegregated schools, few have been shown to influence African
American student achievement positively (Irvine, 1990). A new wave
of reformers has concluded that

> we must abandon the pretense that urban school districts are functioning
> systems that can deliver equal opportunities if relatively simple interven-

tions—cross-district desegregation plans, magnet schools, better court supervision, more money, etc.—are put in place. (Fossey, 1998, p. 16)

In this chapter, we explore ways of broadening the foundations for
teacher education to include a more explicit emphasis on the African
American education tradition. The African American tradition, which
emphasizes care, community, and justice, as discussed in the previous
chapter, provides an important foundation for creating just and caring
learning environments in postdesegregation urban schools (see also
Dempsey & Noblit, 1993; Irvine & Irvine, 1983; Noblit, 1993; Siddle
Walker, 1996; Ward, 1995). Indeed, it is time to explore ways of integrating this tradition into teacher education programs, especially programs situated in urban universities (Cadray, 2001). We begin this
chapter by considering specifically what desegregation policy left out:
preservation of the African American tradition of education. Second,
we examine an intervention within a historically White, urban, public
university (which we call Southland City University) that was in the
process of reaching a desegregation agreement with a neighboring, historically Black, public university. In this intervention, Joseph Cadray
helped teacher educators better understand the lives and experiences
of African American children. Joseph acted as an "interventionist,"
to bring about change. Finally, we discuss how the foundations of
teacher education can be expanded to include the African American
tradition and research strategies. Perhaps through teacher education,
desegregation can be partly reformed.

DESEGREGATION RECONSIDERED

The desegregation of public schools began in the southern United
States after the 1954 Supreme Court's *Brown v. Board of Education*
decision, which ruled that de jure systems of separate but equal schools
were in violation of the Constitution. This decision preceded 15 years
of resistance in most southern states and was implemented only after
subsequent court action. The first desegregation decisions began with
the process of redefining enrollment boundaries for particular school
buildings so that racial balance would improve in schools that had
formerly been racially isolated. This process involved increasing the
use of busing, since neighborhoods were often segregated, and recon-
figuring schools in different ways to make it easier to achieve a racial
equilibrium (e.g., mandating K–2 and 3–6 schools to replace the formerly segregated K–6 schools).

The second wave of school desegregation involved litigation against "de facto" segregation, or systems of education in northern cities that were segregated by patterns of housing rather than on the philosophy of separate but equal. To desegregate northern cities, educators and public officials introduced new structural mechanisms, including magnet schools, to the arsenal of strategies used by the courts. In these venues, the focus of the courts shifted to finding ways to compel more families to choose diverse schools for their children.

However, although the desegregation mandates were usually implemented in ways similar to what had been prescribed by the courts, these remedies did not lead to the integration of schools, especially urban schools (Fossey, 1998; Orfield, Frankenberg, & Lee, 2002; Teddlie, 1998). By *integration*, we mean the affirmative processes of balancing races within educational institutions and creating just and caring learning environments for diverse children. Many financially comfortable Whites either moved to the suburbs or enrolled their children in private schools. This movement—the "great White flight"—reflects what Kohlberg would call a preconventional attitude toward the new laws. The laws, that is, were seen by White parents as not serving their personal interests, so they had no obligation to abide by them.

Today, in a growing number of U.S. cities, desegregation has come to a legal end (e.g., Indianapolis and Boston); the courts are concluding that certain urban school districts are now desegregated; and we are entering a postdesegregation period in most urban communities. But, as courts back away from desegregation, inner-city schools often remain racially isolated. This new pattern is ironic, given that urban educators increasingly work in racially isolated schools that courts have designated as "desegregated."

To complicate the portrait of racial isolation, in pursuit of excellence during the past 2 decades, federal and state educational policies have placed a greater emphasis on standardized tests, national educational standards, and the alignment of curricula and standards. Further, many of the urban universities have attempted to provide teacher education aimed at responding to national and state reform initiatives, including the new "excellence" mandates, without explicitly considering the educational needs of urban children (Tompkins, 2003). Yet in the postdesegregation urban context, we need more educators to consider the learning needs of African American children who attend supposedly desegregated urban school systems. Slaughter-Defoe and Carlson (1997) found that African American third graders from urban areas high in poverty viewed teacher-child relations as the most important aspect of school climate; these children valued caring teachers who listened to students and were available to comfort and help with school and personal problems. Specifically, the ethic of care that was once central to African American schooling, but was almost lost as a result of desegregation, should be intentionally revived and nurtured within contemporary school contexts.

African American Teaching and Learning Traditions

Research indicates that the African American education tradition places a strong emphasis on care and community, qualities that were enhanced in schools controlled by African Americans (Irvine & Irvine, 1983; Ward, 1995). The evolution of this tradition in the context of school desegregation merits more attention. In particular, we are struck by the contrasting images: (1) the caring community in a segregated Black high school in North Carolina before desegregation (Siddle Walker, 1996); (2) the decline in a culture of care in a southern school system as an outgrowth of desegregation (Dempsey & Noblit, 1993); and (3) the re-creation of caring environments in desegregated schools in Louisiana that were involved in the Accelerated Schools Project's democratic restructuring process (St. John, Griffith, & Allen-Haynes, 1997).

First, the concept of care was integral to the concept of quality education in African American schools before desegregation (Irvine & Irvine, 1983; Siddle Walker, 1996). Vanessa Siddle Walker's 1996 study of the history of an exceptional Black high school in North Carolina before desegregation showed a caring school culture. The school not only had teachers with higher levels of education than those of White teachers in surrounding schools, but also had a deep commitment to the development of children and to finding resources in the community for the support of children. For example, in recorded comments, former teachers and students told how the community had allocated funds for the support of the children's travel and for their extensive extracurricular programs. This example illustrates a form of local democracy based on commitment, relationships, and care. However, as a result of desegregation, this high school was transformed into a junior high school and, when integrated, ceased to exhibit these qualities.

Second, the desegregation process systematically ignored conceptions of school quality that have been valued in the African American tradition (Irvine & Irvine, 1983; Dempsey & Noblit, 1993). In a case study of a desegregation process in a southern community, Dempsey & Noblit (1993) examined the different perceptions of what constituted "good" schools for Whites and African Americans. Many African American schools had a strong tradition of teachers working together in ways that demonstrated care and responsibility for the development of children, families, and neighborhoods. In contrast, the White community was more concerned about test scores than about the communal qualities of schools. However, the White community dominated the school board, and the board closed the school that was exemplary by African American standards. The teachers formerly employed by the African American school were released. Dempsey and Noblit (1993) further describe how the closing of the historically African American school led to a decline in the close-knit relationships within the neighborhood that surrounded the former institution.

Third, school restructuring can create a broader conception of education that embraces critical aspects of the African American tradition. Stories of care similar to those described by Siddle Walker and Tompkins (see chapter 4) were also evident in some of the exemplary Accelerated Schools included in a recent study of family involvement in schools (St. John et al., 1997). In one previously African American school, a White teacher described how she had used her church's bus to take poor children (African American and White) from the school on field trips for school activities. An African American parent in the same school described how she had been involved in planning for the pilot test of a conflict-resolution process that had helped create a climate of care on the playgrounds. In another historically African American school, parents described how their neighborhood pride had been raised by the school's multicultural education program. This Accelerated School had also proved more effective at raising achievement scores for nontransient students between third and fifth grade than Accelerated Schools in the same urban area that had not taken a multicultural approach (Slack & St. John, 1999). In a school whose student body was one third African American, an African American teacher commented that she had learned she could care for all children, White as well as Black, as a result of her experience with the Accelerated Schools Project. When teachers began to share their feelings with one another, the racial divisions within schools began to disintegrate (St. John et al., 1997). Thus, caring-and-just communities of educators committed to the development of all children, their families, and neighborhoods had been created in these schools. Arguing for the primacy of such communities for educators, Noddings (1992) reflects that "it is right for students to understand the power of community—that we, as members of a community, act to preserve and improve it; that . . . we bear the marks of the community in which we are raised" (pp. 117–118). In these cases, the model of community was rooted in African American traditions.

This alternative image of the culture of care in the African American tradition is also evident from research on historically Black colleges and universities (HBCUs). A higher percentage of African Americans who choose HBCUs rate their colleges' academic reputations as important and further expect to attain advanced professional and academic degrees than do African Americans who choose to attend largely White colleges (McDonough, Antonio, & Trent, 1997). In addition, many White students who attended HBCUs commented in interviews that the HBCUs were more caring places than the public White campuses they had previously attended (Conrad, Brier, & Braxton, 1997). Thus, a culture of relationship and care seems to be a more integral part of African American education than it is in the majority of educational systems.

Developing an African American Alternative

These examples affirm that, within the African American tradition, a strong culture of care existed that can be built upon in efforts to restructure urban schools (e.g., Comer, Haynes, Joyner, & Ben-Avie, 1996; Finnan, St. John, Solvacek, & McCarthy, 1996). Indeed, this review suggests that it is possible to create just and caring school communities that include important aspects of the African American tradition. The ethic of care and relationship may offer an important balance to the more conventional patterns of academic achievement that dominate the majority schools. The decline in this underlying culture of care in African American schools could also be contributing to the perceptions of problems in the new urban schools.

In the new postdesegregation period, teacher education programs, especially those in urban universities, must incorporate an emphasis on the African American tradition into their curricula (Irvine, 2000; McAllister & Irvine, 2000). Since many urban schools are predominantly African American, emphasis on this tradition may be essential. However, rather than preparing students to understand the centrality of this care ethic, many teacher education strategies draw predominantly on the principles of John Dewey's progressive philosophy of education, which also provides a foundation for the field of moral education. Dewey, the preeminent American philosopher of education in the 20th century, argued for an inquiry-based approach to education improvement, which involved teachers in experiments aimed at improving learning. This focus, while important, is not sufficient to help student teachers understand the postdesegregation contexts in which they will be working and how to work successfully with the students.

Emphasizing the African American educational tradition can help teacher educators bring a better balance of moral education foundations and methods into their teacher education programs. Currently, many teacher educators see their work as being caught between older progressive values and the newer emphasis on excellence and standards. Yet neither the older progressive vision of education nor the newer technocratic vision of educational excellence places a sufficient emphasis on balancing justice and care. Thus, interventions that enable teacher educators to achieve this integration of educational philosophies in teacher education should be a high priority for education reformers.

Our conclusions about the need to broaden the foundations of teacher education and to reform teacher education in urban universities come at a time when teacher education and professional development are in transition. One of the core issues facing urban teacher educators is the following: How can we broaden American teacher education to equip prospective teachers to understand the African American experience in urban schools and best meet the needs of students?

INTERVENING TO FACILITATE UNDERSTANDING OF THE AFRICAN AMERICAN MORAL EXPERIENCE

To test the need to redirect the dialogue in teacher education programs from a preoccupation with the tensions between progressivism and excellence to include an emphasis on the African American educational tradition, we initiated the intervention described below in Southland City University's School of Education.

In this intervention, we used the steps in the intervention process identified by Argyris (1993), but adapted it to deal more directly with the implied social and critical issues. The process involved interviewing participants, organizing and interpreting findings, providing feedback, and facilitating change. Our description of the intervention outlines the context and interview process, the "frames of meaning" (i.e., patterns of logical assumptions regarding teacher education) that were derived from the interviews, and the feedback and change sessions. Because this intervention involved posing moral dilemmas to teacher educators, which enabled them to ponder the moral foundations for their teaching practices, the intervention can also be viewed as a moral education process.

Setting for the Intervention

An African American male teacher educator working in a historically White, urban, public university, Joseph Cadray, initiated the intervention at Southland City University (SCU), located in a southern state that had once operated a de jure system of segregated public education and of segregated urban universities. SCU was situated in a county populated mostly by African Americans and located near a historically Black college that also prepares teachers. This situation limited Black enrollment in the SCU School of Education. A majority of Whites, mostly middle-income females from surrounding counties, were enrolled in the SCU School of Education.

This state and the United States Department of Justice reached a compromise agreement designed to bring the dual state systems of higher education to an end in 1981. Under the weight of the desegregation agreement and administrative espousal of an urban mission for the university, the SCU education faculty began to project a public image, through written texts, that portrayed the college as a participant in the creation of a more just and integrated educational system in Southland City. This did not mean that each SCU education faculty member significantly altered his or her professional practices in response to the just intent of the urban mission ideal. Given the fact that the urban mission was greatly influenced by the desegregation agreement and other contextual factors, the faculty could have responded in ways that would merely project a superficial commitment to the culturally diverse needs of Southland City. Within this context, Cadray formed the hypothesis that a considerable gap may have existed between the stated mission of the SCU School of Education and the traditional person-centered ways in which the faculty seemed to be framing their individual and collective teacher-preparation practices. Publicly acknowledging his intent to test that hypothesis, Cadray initiated the change process while serving on a committee organized to enhance the SCU undergraduate teacher-preparation curriculum.

Members of the Curriculum and Instruction Department's Teacher Preparation Committee (hereafter referred to as *the committee*) participated in this study during the mission-driven period of curricular enhancement within the School of Education. The committee was composed of two full professors (Craven and Carol), one assistant professor (Juliana), and three college instructors (Jane, Nell, and Joseph). Craven, Carol, Jane, and Nell are European Americans. Juliana and Joseph are African Americans.

First, Joseph interviewed the members of the committee. Their perceptions were analyzed and presented back to the committee members to facilitate a dialogue in feedback and change sessions (Cadray, 1995, 1997).

The Initial Frames of Teacher Educators

In the study, the assumptions used by committee members to designate the problems inherent to change were referred to as their "frames." The committee process was ideal for gathering data that could be used to describe and analyze the frames used by those faculty.

The general and specific assumptions that underlie traditional (person-centered) and alternative (group-centered) frames of teacher preparation are summarized in Figure 5. The traditional person-centered and alternative community-centered assumptions were used to make judgments about the frames used by the committee members to construct the SCU teacher education curriculum and their own professional practices. In one sense, the alternative frames represent a critique of moral education as it is traditionally defined. However, they also may represent a more mature form of moral reasoning. Consider this general assumption common to the alternative frames: "The social context of schooling and higher education is dynamic and problematic. Elimination of structural inequities in social systems through collective action should be the primary focus of change efforts." This assumption is highly compatible with the foundational assumptions of moral education, which emphasize the utilization of open discussion of moral dilemmas to facilitate moral development (Higgins, 1995; Snarey, 1992). Further, the emphasis on eliminating inequalities is consonant with postconventional ethical principles, as discussed by Kohlberg (1981, 1984). Thus, by allowing the alternative frame to direct the traditional frames already manifest in teacher educators' practices, interventionists can sharpen the moral foundations used by educators in a manner compatible with the spirit of moral education.

Committee members' initial frames of understanding suggested that the theories used to prepare teachers were grounded primarily in traditional assumptions. These findings seemed to further support the hypothesis that there was a gap between the urban mission and the practice of teacher educators. From this vantage point, committee

FIGURE 5. Teacher Educators' Theoretical Frames

Person-Centered Frames		
General Framing Assumptions		
The social context of schooling and higher education is static and given. The individual teacher candidate should be the primary focus of change efforts.		
Specific Framing Assumptions		
Technical	*Academic*	*Developmental*
Learning to teach involves mastery of predetermined knowledge, skills, and competencies derived from teacher-effectiveness research.	Learning to teach involves acquisition of knowledge in core disciplines of the liberal arts and sciences.	Learning to teach involves active participation in one's own learning, communication with children during early field experiences, and an understanding of children's growth and development.
Research-based competencies are related to the "job" of teaching, and the teacher is the executor of the effective teaching principles.	The teacher's role is subject-matter specialist.	Teacher preparation is best when it promotes the personal development of prospective teachers.
Competence is determined by performance of predetermined competencies, which are assumed to be related to pupil learning.	Improvement of teaching competencies requires more academic course work.	Individual teacher development includes coming to terms with self, maximizing a sense of self-efficacy, clarifying values, and discovering their own meaning and teaching style.
The basic teacher-training model includes (a) learning theory behind the technique, (b) observing a demonstration of the technique, (c) practicing the technique and getting feedback, and (d) getting help from a coach who can detect errors and point to correct behaviors.	Research on subject-matter pedagogy informs both teacher preparation and change initiatives.	

FIGURE 5. (continued)

Community-Centered Frames		
General Framing Assumptions		
The social context of schooling and higher education is dynamic and problematic. Elimination of structural inequities in social systems through collective action should be the primary focus of change efforts.		
Specific Framing Assumptions		
Single-Group Studies	*Multicultural Education*	*Multicultural and Social Reconstruction*
Learning to teach requires a sufficient understanding of the history and cultural background of specific cultural groups.	Learning to teach involves learning to look beyond traditional lenses to see the context of classroom interactions and processes enacted by teachers and students as individuals and members of social groups.	Learning to teach involves learning to promote social change toward greater social, educational, economic, and political equity among diverse cultural groups.
Most textbooks are White and male dominated and treat other groups in a fragmented manner.	Educational change involves changing the entire schooling process, particularly reorganizing the curriculum content around the viewpoints and knowledge of different cultural groups.	Teachers must incorporate four elements into their teaching: actively practice classroom democracy, require students to analyze their circumstances, teach social-action skills, and promote partnerships among diverse groups.
Core discipline knowledge should be reconceptualized based on the experiences and perspectives of previously silenced groups.		
Knowledge about a specific group's oppression will raise people's consciousness concerning social inequity.		

members' traditional practices appeared to be partially responsible for the inadequate preparation of SCU's education graduates for service in culturally diverse settings.

The Intervention Process

The interventionist initiated a reflective intervention process designed to influence the "reframing" (altering assumptions through open dialogue) of the traditional frames that had been assimilated by SCU committee members and to construct a revised teacher-preparation curriculum and recommend personal practices. To facilitate reframing, two reflective sessions, a feedback session in June 1993 and a change session in July 1993, were conducted with committee members. Both reflective sessions were tape-recorded for retrospective analysis. At each of these sessions, only one committee member was not present.

During the feedback session, the interventionist explained his perception of a mission-practice gap and read from selected literature to stimulate inquiry among committee members. He provided such feedback to assess the reactions of committee members to his findings.

After reviewing the data for a few minutes, two of the three practitioners offered immediate reflections on how they framed their practices to prepare teachers. Craven conceded that he was "very naive about multicultural education." He recognized that his way of viewing the "preparation of teachers . . . [was] not basically that much different . . . [for] any population." Then Jane commented that she had already adjusted her practices by incorporating multicultural strategies into her methods. She assumed that teaching her students about the importance of "being sensitive to students' needs [and] being able to incorporate a variety of learning styles [and having] a lot of interpersonal skills" was sufficient to prepare teachers to teach in culturally diverse settings. Jane also responded that some multicultural strategies, such as the celebration of ethnic holidays and training in interpersonal skills, had already been incorporated into the members' traditional frames. Nell did not offer an immediate response to the feedback data, which at this point appeared to have little effect on the committee members' lack of understanding in regard to the unintended consequences that might result from the traditional way they framed the curriculum and their practices in it.

As the feedback session progressed, the members demonstrated an initial awareness of the possible need to consider alternative frames. For example, after reflecting more deeply, Craven and Nell were able to identify literature they had read recently that suggested that greater emphasis should be placed on the preparation of teachers to negotiate diversity and inequality in the schools. However, the committee members' traditional framing assumptions, which excluded attention to various intersections of inequity, remained dominant and out of reach for critical examination.

The second intervention session, the change session, was held 2 weeks after the feedback session. In this session, the interventionist provided an opportunity for committee members to react publicly to the feedback data, which included transcripts of conversations from the feedback session. The interventionist's primary goal for the change session was to influence the committee members, through reflective communication, to construct a teacher-preparation program in which teachers would exhibit greater care and responsibility for SCU teaching graduates and the children they taught in diverse cultural settings.

Committee members had 2 weeks before the change session to reflect on the feedback data. At the change session, after a brief phase of clarification questions, most members (except Juliana) were reunited as they entered the strategic mode. Jane, Craven, and Nell, however, attempted to deflect responsibility for the mission-practice gap onto a variety of factors beyond their control. Arguments that were discussed included the following: (1) most SCU education students did not want to be prepared to teach in Southland County; (2) the needs of less diverse counties were important—other counties collectively took priority in their preparation of students to enter schools; and (3) economic conditions hampered the recruitment and preparation of candidates who did want to teach in Southland County. While these arguments were raised and discussed, critical inquiry into the consequences of committee members' almost exclusive adherence to traditional framing assumptions was effectively postponed.

Later in the change session, the committee members also demonstrated reflective thinking about the diversity challenge as members who interacted during the change session underwent a distinct, observable shift and began to examine the underlying consequences of their collective choices and actions relative to the mission-practice gap. The development of members' understanding about the limitations of their traditional frames can be seen through the kinds of inquiries that emerged. They began to question how to build a better understanding of the urban situation that students who graduated from the program might face, as well as how they might better educate students to enter these settings with a greater sense of the African American tradition of care.

The development of this capacity for collective self-reflection was facilitated by an important change in the committee members' reactions after the feedback session. Although they had devised further rationalization and defensive strategies between the two intervention sessions, committee members had also obviously wrestled internally with the morally problematic mismatch between the sociocultural context that enveloped the college mission and the personal choices they had made relative to teacher preparation. Given the time to reflect between the sessions, members developed the capacity to talk more openly about the nontraditional preparatory needs of prospective teachers. For example, they communicated that "some of our students go in looking for something to support their prejudices." They also talked about how some students had "no idea that there were [rundown] buildings like that . . . called schools." Committee members referred to an article in *Education Leadership*, "How Do We Prepare Teachers to Improve Race Relations?" (B. E. Cross, 1993), as they recognized and communicated about the limitations of traditional frames in relationship to addressing these sociocultural realities.

The development of this collective capacity made it easier for committee members to talk about the educational patterns that could be changed to further centralize the caring aspect of the teacher-preparation curriculum. As deflective behaviors virtually disappeared during the latter phase of the change session, members talked about the frustration of students in inner-city field placements. For example, Nell was able to share her personal reflection on what happens to some of her students who teach in predominantly African American schools. She explained how some students might assert that the lesson they had given "was wonderful" or might praise a "cute little book," which usually resulted in Nell's pointing out that "the lessons and books didn't have any effect at all on those kids you are working with."

A deepening awareness of personal framing assumptions and dialogue about the limitations of traditional patterns of practice enabled committee members to begin inquiry into alternative teacher-preparation frames. In response to conversations about the inadequacy of the preparation of prospective teachers to deal with cross-racial issues, Jane posed a question that exemplified an emerging capacity to facilitate and encourage committee members to think about teacher preparation from alternative perspectives. She asked, "How can we get them thinking about those things before the field experiences?"

Committee members then brainstormed several possible alternatives for enhancing the multicultural strength of the preparation offered to SCU education undergraduates. They considered such options as a required undergraduate multicultural course with content-specific threads running through the curriculum, portfolios for reflecting on feelings and beliefs about culturally diverse groups, and efforts to increase dialogue on racial and diversity issues with Southland County teachers.

The committee members also debated ways of making the African American tradition more central to discussions about equipping teachers in their subsequent meetings during the remainder of the academic year. Nell suggested that one place to facilitate continued discussion was at school field placements. She said when students "have to write a reflection . . . that's where we can get to that discussion." Jane also recognized that such dialogue ought to occur and suggested that it should take place "when our students go into those classrooms and they interact with those [African American] teachers in the classrooms."

Through deepening personal insights and open dialogue, committee members recognized that they had been repeating dysfunctional patterns by exclusively employing traditional framing assumptions. They began to take deliberate action to facilitate alternative teacher preparation. For example, in sharing a classroom experiment with the committee, Juliana exclaimed, "I can see a change in me and it happened just . . . last night . . . after our [committee] meeting. My little multicultural lesson changed . . . it was my awareness of the stronger [alternative] multicultural strategies that made us directly focus on them." Juliana also said that her class discussion covered a variety of diversity issues, including race relations, the homogeneity of the teacher-candidate pool, and how the "traditional structure of schooling and higher education may be perpetuating social inequality."

In these meetings, committee members shared new understandings that emerged as a result of deep reflection on personal assumptions and experiences in light of their increased awareness of alternative framing assumptions. In addition, they honed a capacity to shape a teacher-preparation program that will effectively engender a greater demonstration of care and a greater willingness to act responsibly toward SCU students and the children they teach in culturally diverse settings.

CONCLUSION: EXPAND TEACHER EDUCATION TO INCLUDE AFRICAN AMERICAN TRADITIONS

In our view, the intervention process in the SCU committee had the effect of broadening the discussion among SCU teacher educators to include caring about the voices and experiences of African American students. These teacher educators embodied a transformation in their articulation of how their educational dynamics intricately involved the lives and learning of urban African American students. Rather than communicating continuing loyalty to "race-neutral" and traditional theories, in their discussions they gradually opened themselves to complex issues involved in the experiences of African American children in inner-city schools. Although this response needs to be further tested in practice, we think these developments helped create a learning environment that can have ripple effects by educating teachers to become more aware of the African American tradition.

The process of intervening in urban schools and schools of education to facilitate discussion of the foundations used in educational practice represents a democratic, moral education process for educators. Discussing moral dilemmas that foster conversation about alternative educational practices can provide a framework for actively responding to injustices faced by African American children and can support mature moral thinking among teacher educators.

The idea that the African American education tradition provides a conceptual foundation that can inform the development of teacher education programs in urban universities and perhaps guide a new wave of innovations in urban schools is now little more than a vision. However, like most visions, this notion alone does not depict the practical and tactical aspects of realizing the vision. Therefore, we conclude by identifying some of the ways that future interventions and investigations might contribute to building a better understanding of this possibility. There are three types of actions that teachers, teacher educators, and university researchers can take to move closer to this vision.

First, more teacher educators in urban schools of education need to reflect openly and collectively on the foundations for their teacher education programs. Although the research evidence on the African American education tradition (Siddle Walker, 2000) is limited, it is also compelling. Historically, education faculty such as Lawrence Kohlberg (1981, 1984) sought universal foundations for the theories that are used to guide teacher education. We do not discount this Western philosophical tradition, but rather acknowledge that contributors to feminist, critical, and African American theories not only add to these philosophical foundations, but also perceive the pervasive need for care that dominates urban schools. At the very least, more faculty in urban schools of education need to explore what it means to integrate diverse perspectives into the foundations and methods they use in their classrooms. Part 1 of this volume provides several compelling chapters that foster critical thinking about the African American tradition.

Second, a more fundamental challenge involves integrating a better understanding of African American tradition into school restructuring processes. Other than Comer's school development process (Comer et al., 1996), most of the widely accepted restructuring methods do not include an explicit emphasis on the African American tradition. However, this approach may be integrated into other restructuring processes, including the Accelerated Schools Project (Miron, St. John, & Davidson, 1998). Allowing the African American tradition to lay foundations for the restructuring process can lead to meaningful, and psychologically significant, improvements in student outcomes (Slack & St. John, 1999). Through this type of experimentation process, it will be possible to create a larger number of just and caring schools that can be visited by aspiring educators and studied by educational researchers.

Third, research that examines the meaning of the African American tradition in education should be expanded. More historical research is needed on schools that have closed or changed as a result of desegregation. Likewise, studies that examine the new efforts to integrate the African American tradition into teacher education programs and school restructuring processes are important. For example, it is critical to examine whether a new moral foundation does emerge, one that emphasizes both justice and care, as well as whether these experiments have lasting effects on students and school communities. Finally, the relationship between these experiments and learning outcomes for children in urban schools needs more exploration.

In conclusion, this chapter has raised a set of questions about the role of teacher education institutions in developing teachers who have an appreciation for the African American caring tradition. If urban schools of education entered a period of experimentation with more balanced approaches to the justice of desegregated environments and the care that permeated the segregated environment, they could help bring more balance to our collective understanding of meaningful integration. Indeed, schools that value the voices of African American children can also be more welcoming to Whites (Conrad et al., 1997). Through a broadening of the foundations of teacher education in urban schools of education to include African American conceptions of justice and care, more inclusive learning environments may be created for all children.

CHAPTER 6

Crime and Punishment: Moral Dilemmas in the Inner-City Classroom

Jennifer E. Obidah, Marquita Jackson-Minot, Carla R. Monroe, and Brian Williams

> If you can show me how I can cling to that which is real to me, while teaching me a way into the larger society, then I will not only drop my defenses and my hostility, but I will sing your praises and I will help you to make the desert bear fruit.
>
> —Ralph Ellison, *Going to the Territory*

A MERICA'S SCHOOLS have traditionally been assigned much of the responsibility for shaping the morality of the nation's youth. Beginning with the "dame" schools, created in the homes of "well-respected women" during North America's colonial era, instruction was designed not only to teach reading, writing, and arithmetic, but, equally or more important at the time, also to provide moral education. Teaching included explicit ethical instruction based on Christian values and implicit moral guidance based on the teacher's life as a role model (Cuban, 1993; Sadker & Sadker, 1997). Today, schools continue to attempt to provide an education in morality for their students, but much has changed.

Currently, in addition to moral and religious education being separated from each other, explicit and implicit moral teachings are presented independently. Explicitly, reasoning about moral issues is often addressed, but rather than being integrated into the academic curriculum, it is "ghettoized" in particular areas of the curriculum, such as

civics or character education courses (DeHaan, Hanford, Kinlaw, Philler, & Snarey, 1997). Implicitly, much of moral education has become
part of the hidden curriculum, where it is unacknowledged but conveyed subtly through teacher-student interactions (Hansen, 2002) and
school policies (Strike, Haller, & Soltis, 1998). Over the past decade,
however, increasing social problems in the community have challenged the adequacy of these approaches to promoting the moral development of students, especially as questionable moral values are
conveyed through school policies.

This is especially true in the case of schools that serve economically disadvantaged students who live in inner cities where violence
has become a daily reality that affects the lives of many urban youth
(Hart, Atkins, & Ford, 1998; Monroe, 2003). Residents in the inner
cities are crime victims twice as often as those who live in suburban
areas. Yet "there has been only limited attention to psychological impacts of victimization," and even less attention to "covictimization,"
which involves the psychological trauma of directly witnessing a violent act (cf. Kuther & Wallace, 2003; Ladd & Cairns, 1996; Warner &
Weist, 1996, p. 362).

Violence within school also has become a central concern (Centers for Disease Control and Prevention, 1996; Elam & Rose, 1995;
Furlong, Chung, Bates, & Morrison, 1995; Noguera, 1995; Rose, Gallup, & Elam, 1997). Simply stated, many students and teachers are
afraid to go to school for fear of being harmed. Well-publicized shoot-
ings on school grounds have further intensified public concern over
school violence (Bragg, 1997; Gegax, Adler, & Pedersen, 1998; Hays,
1998; Witkin, Tharp, Schrof, Toch, & Scattarella, 1998). Efforts to control school violence now include the use of metal detectors, electronic
monitoring systems, security guards, and police officers (Astor, Meyer
& Behre, 1999), although studies have suggested that such approaches
are not effective (Forst & Blomquist, 1991; Morrison, Furlong, & Morrison, 1997; Schneider & Schramm, 1986). More punitive measures
and alternative policies are also being tried to reduce the incidence of
violence among students.

Pressed by public opinion, many urban schools have adopted
"zero tolerance" approaches to school violence and criminal activities
(Noguera, 1995). Students found in violation of specific school policies, such as a ban on the possession of controlled substances or weapons, are immediately expelled. Such consequences are assumed to
teach students not only that certain acts involving crime, violence,
and drug use are prohibited on school property, but also that the offenses will be punitively answered with expulsion.

Often, these rules do serve the purpose of providing students and staff with safe and orderly environments in which effective teaching and learning can occur. Still, the moral reasoning that is being conveyed through these policies amounts to little more than a kind of behavior management. If students do violate any of the imperatives, policies such as zero tolerance dictate that schools will offer no empathy, exceptions, or options. These zero tolerance policies provide a good example of what Kohlberg would identify as conventional, rather than principled, justice reasoning. All students are expected to abide by explicit rules; justice is defined as the uncompromising enforcement of these rules; and the school system is understood as being ethical when it is orderly.

The strict adherence to such school rules and policies means that there is no space for education professionals to consider extenuating circumstances that invariably arise. Moreover, the role of teachers in shaping the moral reasoning of the student becomes more limited as they themselves are silenced by such policies (Garbarino, Kostelny, & Dubrow, 1991). Challenges arise when the moral message implicit in a policy such as zero tolerance conflicts with the best interests of students. From a developmental perspective, students would increasingly avoid crime and violence as they developed the ability to reason in ethically mature ways about these activities. Promoting such development would enable students to willingly advance the safety and welfare of themselves and their fellow human beings.

This chapter focuses on the dilemmas inherent in the zero tolerance policy. Although gun violence clearly affects young people from all socioeconomic and racial backgrounds, here we will focus exclusively on violence that affects economically disadvantaged African American children attending inner-city schools. In particular, we examine how and why an ethic of care-and-justice, as opposed to an exclusive focus on an ethic of justice, must be included when teachers are confronted with moral decisions. Such an ethic is vital in a "society like ours where so much depends on success in school" and where "children not only need continuous love and warm companionship from adults" but "also need adults who can present the world effectively" (Noddings, 1995, p. 672).

We present a scenario that occurs in an inner-city classroom and involves a teacher and a student. This scenario is based upon factual events, as well as on teacher and student conversations taken from a number of research articles and ethnographic studies (Alleyne Johnson, 1995; Diver-Stamnes, 1995; Noguera, 1995; Obidah, 2000). We follow this with a discussion of the ethics of justice and care as they relate to the teacher's moral reasoning. We then examine why justice must be tempered by care and conclude that a context of caring may be a more appropriate way for teachers to interact initially with students who are struggling with life circumstances in which violence, substance abuse, and other dysfunctions are the norm.

A SNAPSHOT OF ONE URBAN CLASSROOM

Ms. Jones strides quickly through the door of her first-period sixth-grade classroom. This is her 6th year teaching middle school, but she still feels excited about teaching today's unit on contemporary American literature. In preparation for today's class she has selected several books that she thinks will speak to her students. Initially tough to connect with, this year's class has turned out to be her favorite and most challenging group of students.

The morning bell rings and the students file into the room in an unusually slow and quiet manner. Ms. Jones meets each one inside the door with a smile and "Good morning." After settling the students and checking attendance, she moves to the front of the class and begins the day's lesson: "All right, let's get started. As I told you on Friday, we're starting a new unit today. We've finished with the grammar lessons we've been working on; so today we're going to start a unit on literature. Now, I've selected a few books I think you'll enjoy, but I also want to get your input and suggestions for other books. What are some things you've read recently?"

She walks to the blackboard, picks up a piece of chalk to make a list, and looks at the class expectantly. The class sits passively, and no one responds. In fact, the students give no indication that they have even heard her question. As Ms. Jones looks over rows of bowed heads, she suddenly understands that the Monday morning blues and low interest in contemporary American literature are not enough to account for the students' eerie silence. She puts the piece of chalk down.

"All right," she says seriously. "What's going on? Is something bothering you?" For the first time, a few students look up, surprised. She tries to read their faces. "Is something wrong? Did something happen?"

"We saw something on the way to school," Tonya, an outspoken 12-year-old, says. "A dead boy."

Ms. Jones is speechless for a moment. Although she is aware of the neighborhood's violent reputation, the announcement still shocks her. "How do I deal with this?" she thinks to herself. Obviously, she cannot continue with the lesson she has planned. Tonya's words hang in the air as an awkward stillness fills the classroom. Still digesting the information, Ms. Jones knows she must face the dilemma. Pulling up a chair and sitting with the students, she says, "Alright. Everyone take out a sheet of paper and write what you're feeling right now. I know this may be hard, but I think it will help if you get it out. Let's write for about 15 minutes, and then talk about it. I'll write too."

Amazed at the depth of feeling that the students' writing reveals, she encourages the class to spend the rest of the period reading their reflection papers and discussing the claim that death has on their lives. Yet it was difficult to conceive of the emotions and circumstances the children faced every morning. Some of the students knew the victim from their neighborhood; others had only seen him in the area. Most of the students had been acquainted with others who had died at a young age as a result of gunshot wounds. These experiences left them angry, afraid, frustrated, anxious, and resigned to the presence of violence and death. Equally disturbing, while the students were aware of how they were victimized by violence, they also believed that sometimes people necessarily had to act outside of accepted rules to get retaliatory "justice." Ms. Jones wonders how she could have overlooked an experience so central to her students' lives. She continues to listen, befuddled, to the discussion.

One student asserts matter-of-factly, "A bullet ain't got nobody's name on it."

Marquis, one of the quieter students, sits up straight in his seat and glares. "Well, sometimes it does have your name on it!" he yells.

"What do you mean, Marquis?" Ms. Jones probes, both surprised and intrigued by his reaction.

"Never mind. Forget it," he says.

"Alright," Ms. Jones replies, trying to keep her composure. "Does anyone else have anything to say?" Ms. Jones moves on and speaks with other students. As the period draws to a close, she walks over to Marquis and asks him to stay awhile after class. His comment in class concerned her, and she wants to understand what he meant.

After some urging, Marquis explains that his father and mother recently separated, and his father had begun to threaten suicide. In a moment of clarity, Marquis's father had instructed his son to remove his 9-mm handgun from the house so that he could not harm himself or anyone else. Not knowing what else to do, Marquis had slipped his father's gun in his backpack and taken it to school with him that morning. The combination of uncertainty about his father and seeing the dead boy that morning had combined to terrify Marquis.

"I just didn't know what else to do," he says wearily.

"I know how you feel," Ms. Jones thinks to herself, for now she is in a similar situation. The school has recently adopted a zero tolerance policy in regard to weapons. If this incident is reported, Marquis will be immediately expelled. Previously, Ms. Jones has enthusiastically supported the policy, which provides students and faculty sanctuary from the violence of the streets. With the morning's death foremost in her mind, she ponders her dilemma. Expulsion will shatter the curious and promising Marquis, and she believes that he is speaking honestly. Yet she certainly agrees that firearms have no place in schools and she believes that she is required by the zero tolerance policy to report the child. Marquis stands vulnerable before her.

"Do you have the gun with you now, Marquis?" He nods and opens his backpack to expose the weapon to his teacher. Ms. Jones stares at the gun, considering what she is about to do. Quickly, she unlocks and opens her desk drawer, lifts the gun with two fingers, places it inside, and closes and relocks the drawer. Marquis, amazed at how swiftly she has relieved him of the gun, feels a small wave of emotional relief.

"Marquis, I understand why you did this," she explains. "But you cannot bring a gun to school. You must not do this ever again. I don't know what's going to happen to you this time. Please, come and see me again after school. We need to talk more about this. I'll see you then." Marquis slowly leaves the room as the following class begins to enter. Ms. Jones sits quietly and considers her situation: She now has a loaded gun in her desk, a very upset student in her class, many difficult questions to resolve, and another class to teach in a few seconds.

AN EXAMINATION OF THE TEACHER'S MORAL DILEMMA

Ms. Jones understands the gravity of her dilemma. Questions about Marquis's future, about her relationship with other students, and about the vocational ramifications of her decision are all critical. She considers how her actions may shape the moral understandings of other students and her own ability to care for the students and protect their rights in future years. Additionally, her coworkers and the principal will be affected by her decision.

Ms. Jones is faced with a severe moral dilemma. "When seen in terms of either care or justice, . . . problems," such as those faced by Marquis and Ms. Jones—"appear to have right, if difficult, answers; seen from both perspectives, however, their ethical ambiguity is obvious" (Brown, Tappan, & Gilligan, 1995, p. 316). African American care-and-justice ethics allows one to acknowledge the clear ambiguity. Thus, the dilemma of Ms. Jones provides a helpful framework for discussion of the strengths and limitations inherent in justice and care.

Ethic of Justice

Lawrence Kohlberg (1981) theorized that individuals develop moral reasoning through a series of six increasingly abstract and comprehensive stages, which focus on the major concerns of justice ethics, including equality, respect for human rights, and procedural fairness. He articulated a very useful vision of justice reasoning in that it reflected the major ethical concerns of democracy. Kohlberg maintained, furthermore, that the stages involved in the development of moral reasoning represent an invariant sequence that progresses toward the same universal ethical principles. This sequence remained true, he held, regardless of the social-class and cultural affiliation of the individual. As he summarized his position, almost "all individuals in all cultures use the same . . . basic moral categories, concepts, or principles, and all individuals in all cultures go through the same order or sequence of gross stages of development, though varying in rate and terminal point of development" (p. 186).

Kohlberg's moral universality claim elicited an overwhelming response from critics. Researchers completed numerous studies that tested the validity of the "universality" assumption across diverse social and cultural settings. Their results have both supported and challenged Kohlberg's initial claim. On balance, however, one can say that Kohlberg did not adequately consider the impact of culture (Johnston, 1997; Puka, 1994a; Simpson, 1974; Snarey, 1985), gender (Gilligan, 1982; Noddings, 1988), social class (Snarey, 1995), or race (Johnston, 1997; Vozzola, 1997) upon moral values, moral development, or moral education.

Kohlberg's assertions that equality and reciprocity are ideals toward which all people should move is a useful frame through which to view this dilemma. Within this moral standpoint lies the hope that, despite differences in gender, race, culture, and social class, everyone will be treated fairly (Ward, 1991). A zero tolerance policy in schools, for example, appears impartial and fair because it applies to everyone. Kohlberg's ideal was that the rules of justice are agreed upon by members of society in order to serve the welfare of the whole as well as that of each person in it. He coined the phrase *just community*, to describe such a society; when that ideal is applied to education, it results in what Kohlberg called just community schools. As opposed to the traditional governance structure in which administrators and faculty alone decide and enforce the moral standards for the school, just community schools involve students in developing community and making moral decisions (Blakeney & Blakeney, 1996; Kuhmerker, 1991). But, of course, the school being discussed in this example is not organized as a just community.

Within Marquis's school-community context, numerous obstacles are faced when applying a predetermined set of rules. Although assumed to be universally applicable responses to the problem of violence in educational systems, these rules reflect what Lawrence Kohlberg would call a conventional understanding of morality, because they do not take into account the unique extenuating circumstances of a given "crime." On the other hand, caring for others, only, is not the most mature form of care (Gilligan, 1982). Ms. Jones holds in balance the tension between the kind of moral reasoning represented in an unquestioning enforcement of rules and the moral reasoning represented in a fair and caring consideration for the individual student's human rights and well-being.

Children such as Marquis are routinely expelled for offenses such as bringing a firearm to school. Most people would assert the legitimacy of the school's position. The zero tolerance policy is clear: If you bring a gun to school, you will be expelled. Enforcing the zero tolerance policy unequivocally conveys to all students that the values, laws, and rules of society are meant to protect the well-being of the community and to promote justice. In the abstract, the policy is an unambiguous and unbiased method of eradicating the problem of guns in schools. However, the flaw in this approach is that lives are not lived abstractly. They take place on streets with particular names and in houses with particular conflicts, and sometimes circumstances force the members of that house to willingly or unwillingly break the rules.

People who function at higher stages of moral reasoning do take into account extenuating circumstances, according to Kohlberg (1981). For example, in Marquis's case, there could be little competition between the prospects of enduring the consequences of breaking school rules and of enduring the consequences of not having prevented his father's suicide. Marquis's decision was reached for life-and-death's sake. In his moral agency, he acted to save his father's life. Even at Kohlberg's Stage 4—social maintenance—supporting families is just as essential as punishing lawbreakers in order to preserve an orderly society. At Kohlberg's Stage 5—prior rights and social contract—the person is aware of rights and values that are prior to social attachments and upon which social arrangements are grounded. Thus, from a justice perspective, one could maintain that Marquis should not be punished because the school policy can be seen as serving a lesser value than Marquis's aim of saving his father's life.

The difficulty in this dilemma is not simply the conceptualization of justice, but also its implementation. When conflicts in moral reasoning arise, these conflicts inevitably create dilemmas for those individuals charged with the duty of enforcing the rules and regulations of the greater community. Ms. Jones is faced with such a dilemma. Applying the reasoning that "rules are rules" to Marquis's situation leaves little room for legitimate deviations. If school policies are to be truly effective, faculty and administrators must labor to understand the complex ways in which the children they teach are affected by their communities.

Because disenfranchised groups are often categorized by themselves and others as living on the periphery of society, they may develop moral ideologies that, while structurally similar to other ideologies at Stage 4 in Kohlberg's scheme, differ dramatically in content from what is demanded by the mainstream. At times, their lives are governed by a system of rules or "codes of conduct" that do not fit into the conventional system of norms forged in the mainstream (Canada, 1995; Ward, 1991). For others, the types of moral reasoning that undergird these codes of conduct are necessarily laden with what, in Kohlberg's model, are lower-stage-like tools for self-preoccupation, survival, and even revenge. In reality, inner-city children need these survival kits because mainstream institutions have often failed to protect and provide for them. Evaluated on its own merit, inner-city reasoning fulfills a vital, pragmatic purpose. However, when decontextualized and evaluated by a set of criteria that are not sensitive to the special concerns of life in the inner city, this syllogism suddenly becomes an indication of lower-order reasoning skills and an inferior level of moral development.

More specifically, the dilemma faced by Ms. Jones, when analyzed through a conventional ethic of justice, asserts the need for a reevaluation of morality as it is currently presented in mainstream American society's mores—that is, undergirded by an assumption of universality without consideration of specific contextual differences. Although moral reasoning should be shaped and nurtured in every child, Ms. Jones and the school system must carefully and deliberately identify the best possible course of action in Marquis's situation. In keeping with the view that educators, whether they like it or not, teach values and moral reasoning to their students (Hansen, 2002; Heft, 1995, Kohlberg, 1981), we will discuss the usefulness and limitations of Gilligan's (1982) ethic of care.

Ethic of Care

Carol Gilligan (1982) was one of the first scholars to challenge openly the previously accepted views of moral development grounded in Kohlberg's ethic of justice. She contended that a moral voice exists that is not adequately represented by the justice-focused model. Because Kohlberg's stage theory is the result of research conducted only with White males, she and her colleagues argued that his theories were not an accurate reflection of the development of moral reasoning in women (Gilligan, 1982, 1988; Gilligan, et al., 1988) or African Americans (Eugene, 1989; Ward, 1988). Furthermore, in her research Gilligan questioned the assumption that the highest stage of moral reasoning was based exclusively on objective rationality and universal principles of detached justice. She believed, instead, that legitimate moral and ethical choices were also based on norms of care, human connectedness, and relationships (Gilligan, 1988; Eaker-Rich & Van Galen, 1996). In addition to creating a second major paradigm in the field of moral development, Gilligan's work has brought attention to the effects of power, oppression, and subordination on the development of morality in society.

Gilligan (1982) defines an ethic of care as "the ideals of human relationship, the vision that the self and others will be treated as of equal worth, that despite differences in power, things will be fair; the vision that everyone will be responded to and included, that no one will be left alone or hurt" (p. 63). The ethic of care that Gilligan endorses contains three basic elements. The first is the need to understand and interpret the beliefs and behaviors of members of a given group on their own terms rather than within a paradigm or framework that was not originally based on that population. Thus, the likelihood of misinterpreting or unfairly categorizing a person or group is lessened, and instead, a more accurate, balanced, and fair portrayal of the individual or group may be obtained.

The second element within an ethic of care is the special attention that is given to the role of interpersonal relationships. To Gilligan (1982), these relationships form the cornerstone of the theory because to develop morally, people must shift their focus from personal needs to a concern for others. In particular, an emphasis is placed on compassion and on identifying situations in which the potential to hurt others is minimized. This is important because the manner in which people behave and function is partially influenced by those with whom they interact.

The third element of Gilligan's ethic of care is a promotion of the need to recognize differences without assigning value judgments. This is necessary, she maintains, because it promotes a "non-hierarchical vision of human connection that clarifies that experience" (p. 62). In essence, a sense of pluralism is promoted in which the gifts of each human being are appreciated (Kallen, 1956; Locke, 1935). Moreover, this allows us to better understand the manner in which we are all connected and interdependent. Interpersonal interconnectedness and response to need are the strengths of the ethic of care. In the ideal of care lies the hope that, despite differences, everyone will be cared for, acknowledged, included, and respected. The associated moral concerns tend to focus on problems of detachment, disconnection, abandonment, and indifference (Ward, 1991) and the development of solutions that encompass and alleviate such problems. As shown in the preceding discussion, Gilligan's ethic of care is clearly applicable to educational and social institutions that serve children affected by violence and covictimized by other social ills (see Hart, Atkins, & Ford, 1998).

Noddings (1995) concurs that an ethic of care is important in schools and argues that the curriculum ought to center around themes of care. She contends that first, "we should want more from our educational efforts than adequate academic achievement and, second, that we will not achieve even that meager success unless our children believe that they themselves are cared for and learn to care for others" (p. 675). Furthermore, Noddings believes that much can be gained, both academically and personally, if themes of care are incorporated into the curriculum. Gilligan's and Noddings's interpretations of an ethic of care suggest that teachers should make moral decisions that ensure that a high level of regard and interpersonal responsibility is preserved for all students, irrespective of their race or social condition. Ultimately, acts of care ensure that an appreciation for human connection rather than separation is always maintained. A desire to care such as this clearly influences Ms. Jones's concerns about Marquis. Because her relationship with this student has been based on trust, she is able to believe in the truthfulness of his statements and to recognize the complexity of his situation. This allows her to avoid unilateral condemnation of him for breaking rules that exclude an understanding that he is embedded in a context of violence and for violating policies that, indeed, devalue his life.

Yet as a result of Ms. Jones's caring for Marquis and disregarding policy, her care for the whole group—whom she also does indeed care about—could potentially be jeopardized. School policies and institutional practices can undermine as well as support interpersonal care (see chapter 4). Thus, while Ms. Jones's caring for Marquis may be the best approach for Marquis's situation, it does not solve the larger institutional issues confronted by the school. The resolution of this dilemma calls for more than care; it calls for care-and-justice.

Why Justice Must Be Tempered by Care, and Vice Versa

Teachers who work with students like Marquis are placed in a unique position. They are hired to fulfill a given set of responsibilities and are provided with the tools for success in these endeavors through preservice certification programs and professional development courses. Yet many urban teachers' daily realities force them to make decisions regarding matters in which they have no previous experience or training. In a serious moral dilemma, such as the one faced by Ms. Jones, any choice that the teacher makes will have significant implications in the lives of everyone involved.

Because teachers like Ms. Jones work with students whose lives are disproportionately affected by many covictimizing adverse social conditions (e.g., poverty, crime, and discrimination), judgment about their moral decisions must be tempered with an appreciation for the challenges that these students face. Too often, youths living in economically disenfranchised inner-city neighborhoods are forced to negotiate laws presented to them via legal institutions (e.g., the court system or the police) that are inequitable, given the circumstances of their lives (Canada, 1995). This means that even blind-and-equal enforcement of the law, let alone more severe enforcement, does not yield justice for them and often fosters a sense of resentment that becomes ingrained in the social fabric of the life of the community and the consciousness of its residents (Canada, 1995; Prothrow-Stith, 1991). As a result, many residents, particularly young Black males, respond violently to people and institutions that they perceive as agents in their economic and social subjugation (see chapter 3). Yet when these individuals are treated with concern and empathy by members of mainstream society, such as teachers, the experience provides a much needed alternative to what can be a degrading daily reality.

In his analysis of responses to school violence, Noguera (1995) maintains that the "get-tough" approach predominant in schools' responses to violence not only fails to create a safe environment but also interrupts teaching and learning and increases mistrust and resistance. Noguera comments that "it is in the context of fulfilling goals that have traditionally prioritized maintaining order and control over students, as opposed to creating humane environments for learning, that schools have become increasingly susceptible to violence" (p. 191). He asserts the need for alternative, less coercive, strategies, such as conflict-resolution programs, which teach students how to settle disputes nonviolently; mentoring programs that pair students with adult role models; and a variety of counseling programs based on partnerships between schools and social service agencies. Moreover, Noguera advocates that teachers get to know the young people they teach beyond their "student" identity. He notes that teachers' "sense of what their students' lives are like outside of school is either distorted by images of pathological and dysfunctional families, or simply shrouded in ignorance. Fear and ignorance can serve as barriers greater than any fence and can be more insulating than any security system" (p. 204). Thus, although he does not discuss an ethic of care specifically, Noguera's analysis supports the need for an ethic of care in schools that serve students coping with issues such as violence.

Currently, several prevailing educational theories reflect many elements of an ethic of care—cultural synchronization, culturally responsive pedagogy, culturally relevant pedagogy, and cultural congruence (see Irvine, 1990; Ladson-Billings, 1994, 2000; Shade, 1994). One of the most popular theories is culturally responsive teaching. Although she does not specifically address an ethic of care, Ladson-Billings (1994) asserts that culturally responsive teachers consciously work to form strong relationships and connections with their students that affirm the personal and cultural traits the children possess. This entails discovering the commonalities the instructor shares with his or her pupils; encouraging students to have a positive self-concept; and treating each student with respect, kindness, and fairness, irrespective of differences. Additionally, as the teacher comes to know and care for each student, he or she serves as a model for how students should construct their own lives. This helps create an interdependent community in which people feel responsible not only for themselves, but also for one another.

Dialogue that is culturally responsive is a critical component of effective moral education. It is essential from a justice perspective because it allows students to understand democratic decision-making and to gain a first-hand feel for justice (Power et al., 1989; Reimer, Paolitto, & Hersh, 1983). It is essential from a care perspective because "it is a means by which we evaluate the effects of our attempts to care" (Noddings, 1995, p. 191). Additionally, schools and classrooms ought to be places where students and teachers alike are able to share and discuss personal experiences. For students to talk about dilemmas they may face in school and in their communities, the classroom environment must be a safe place where students' and teachers' ideas are listened to and valued (Lamme, 1996). The school and the classroom must be places where "students can reflect on truths and reasons and make moral judgments . . . justice and care should be a major part of the students' moral identities" (Tyree, Vance, & McJunkin, 1997, p. 224).

Noddings (1995) asserts that the benefits of teaching themes of care include (1) expanding the cultural literacy of students, (2) connecting the standard subject areas, (3) connecting students to great existential questions (such as, What is the meaning of life?), and (4) connecting people to other people. Noddings adds that another way in which themes of care can be introduced into classrooms is through teachers being "prepared to respond spontaneously to events that occur in the school or in the neighborhood" (p. 678).

Several examples of educators who have operationalized an ethic of care in their work with students illustrate how these theories can become practices. Obidah, in her teacher's journal, writes about her realization that a connection between school knowledge and real-life issues, including violence and death, was vital for effective teaching and learning to take place in her classroom (Alleyne Johnson [aka, Obidah], 1995). With the help of her students, she sought solutions to the problem this raised. Out of their discussions came the creation of the *Cluster Chronicle*, a newspaper written by and for students. This jointly initiated project became part of the curriculum and was used in conjunction with the "traditional" English course. Importantly, students had joint ownership for their learning as they developed the paper. Additionally, creating a newspaper that was widely read by their peers was empowering for the students. Through the *Cluster Chronicle*, the students engaged the issues of death and violence. In all, eight of the newspaper's articles that year dealt with the role these issues played in the students' lives.

The *Cluster Chronicle* also helped teachers better understand their students' lives and circumstances outside school. Obidah writes that, in the process, she and her students acknowledged their "whole selves, not only the roles of students and teachers" (p. 227). She concludes by describing the changes that had occurred in relationships with her students: "I no longer want to acknowledge students only to the extent of how well they fulfill my expectations or their response to a prescribed, petrified curriculum. I believe that it is not effective or responsible to teach on a day-to-day basis as though nothing that happens outside of the school building impacts on the act of teaching." She continues, "Whether we as teachers choose to address it or not, students' lives come into our classrooms. Instead of wishing for other students, let us gear our work toward the students we have" (pp. 228–229).

Similarly, as a teacher at Medgar Evers High School in the Watts community of southern California, Ann Diver-Stamnes (1995) details her experiences of educating students in an environment severely affected by violence, drug use, teenage pregnancy, and other complications that accompany environments high in poverty. This educator described Watts as a community where "the morbidity and mortality rates are the highest in Los Angeles County; and where the rate of immunization and the number of medical doctors per capita are the lowest" (p. 102). Among the obstacles this educator encountered was the complexity of attempting to teach students who suffered from posttraumatic stress disorder, desensitization, and inequitable educational opportunities in de facto segregated schools.

Diver-Stamnes (1995) also details the obstacle of stress that teachers themselves experienced as a result of teaching in such adverse circumstances. Teachers are universally expected, in the midst of the situation, to enable their students to cope effectively so that they can concentrate on education. Diver-Stamnes comments that teachers like herself, who were involved with their students in Watts, experienced significant stress. She writes, "We often felt we were on the front lines in a war without having been given the weapons to fight the battle" (p. 108). In the midst of such realities, this teacher struggled to increase the possibility of a better life for her students through education. She extended her teaching to encompass and address her students' real-life issues by employing teaching strategies that highlighted the ethic of care that Gilligan (1982) and Noddings (1992) advance. She also extended her teaching to encompass the ethic of justice that Power, Higgins, and Kohlberg (1989) advocate. She did not ignore the justice issues with which her students were dealing, such as inequitable education, fear of crime, police brutality, homicide, and, unsurprisingly for many of them, posttraumatic stress disorder. She addressed some of these problems, for instance, by helping establish a health clinic in the school and by developing peer-counseling programs and referral information for health service agencies, among other strategies (cf. Blakeney & Blakeney, 1992, 1996).

ONGOING REFLECTIONS

Although one teacher alone cannot solve the problems that are intertwined with economic disadvantage, one teacher's affirmation of the value and worth of what urban children have to offer can have enormous effect. By framing decisions within care and justice perspectives, teachers evoke responsibility, offer caring affirmation, and model empathy and fairness. Moreover, a teacher who interacts with his or her students within an ethic of care is a powerful role model in a society that often erroneously equates material possessions with personal human worth.

And yet an individual teacher cannot fully address the problems inherent in this situation. On an interpersonal level, several assumptions are inherent. As mentioned earlier, only Ms. Jones's previous relationship with Marquis has prepared her to determine the level of his honesty. Teachers with less knowledge of their students would be hard pressed in similar encounters to assess reliably a student's actions. Indeed, the crux of interpersonal caring emerges from the desire and skill of the teacher to develop a good relationship with students. Too often, as Irvine indicates (1990), such teacher-student interactions walk on mislaid grounds and misperceptions, especially when cultural differences are unacknowledged.

Moreover, even if the dilemma were resolved in a way that took into account the particular context of Marquis's situation, this resolution would not address the larger structural questions inherent in the zero tolerance policy. For example, why is a zero tolerance policy more common in inner-city schools than in suburban schools, despite the fact that the most publicized forms of school violence have occurred in suburban settings and involved non–African American children? The lack of equity in the implementation of the policy across schools, arguably, is in itself unfair. What kind of institutional message is being transmitted to those students who are most affected by the policy when they listen to stories about White, suburban students who, given free rein, carry weapons to class in their backpacks?

Ms. Jones must voice a concern that schools engage their students with thoughtful, care-based methods inherent in the administration of equity and justice. The situation Ms. Jones has found herself in may be a direct result of the school system's lack of innovative approaches to fostering the kinds of safe environments in which children can thrive.

Return to Ms. Jones's Room

Following Ms. Jones's instructions, Marquis returns to her classroom when the school bell signals the end of the school day. For some time, they talk about the dilemma. Ms. Jones spells out to Marquis how bringing a gun to school is beyond excuse. She tells him that all students who behave similarly should face consequences.

"I know," Marquis replies. "I just didn't know what else to do."

Ms. Jones walks to Marquis, puts her hands on his shoulders, and looks directly at him as she speaks. "Marquis, you were trying to save your father's life. No one can fault you for that. I'm sorry that there are not enough adults in your life that you felt could help you with this problem, but I'm glad that you've allowed me to be one of them."

Resolution One. Ms. Jones continues, "I spoke to the principal at lunch and he's waiting for us in his office. I don't know what the outcome of this will be, but believe me, the principal and I will do everything to make sure that you are treated fairly."

Ms. Jones feels the weight of Marquis's relief as his shoulders visibly relax. Teacher and student walk together to the principal's office. There, the principal and a police officer wait.

Ms. Jones also feels relief, because she believes that this is the fairest solution, but she also has some misgivings because she knows that when the police arrest a young Black male, situations sometimes have a way of blowing up unexpectedly. Following the rules does not necessarily ensure a just solution and, in this case, the rule is zero tolerance.

Resolution Two. Ms. Jones continues, "Let's drive down to the Ohio River and take care of this."

Ms. Jones feels the weight of Marquis's relief as his shoulders visibly relax. Teacher and student walk together to the school's parking lot and drive to the river. There, Ms. Jones and Marquis carefully and discretely drop the paper bag off the side of the bridge and watch it fall and disappear into the deep, muddy waters below.

Ms. Jones feels relieved because she believes that this is the most caring solution to the dilemma, but she also has some misgivings, for she knows that Marquis will still return to a difficult home situation. She worries what other messages she is sending him, and she also knows that secrets have a way of exploding unexpectedly. Breaking the rules does not necessarily ensure a caring solution.

Resolution Three. Ms. Jones continues, "I spoke to the principal at lunch and he's waiting for us in his office. I don't know what the outcome of this will be, but believe me, we—myself, the principal, your mom and dad, yes, we called them in too—we will do everything to make sure that you are treated fairly."

Ms. Jones feels the weight of Marquis's relief as his shoulders visibly relax. Teacher and student walk together to the principal's office. There, Marquis's parents and their pastor, the principal and the school psychologist, and a police officer wait.

Ms. Jones also feels relief, but she still has some misgivings. Her experience reminds her of a moral dilemma she studied in college. Heinz stole a drug to save his wife's life. Should he have to pay the legal consequences of stealing, even though he had accomplished a greater good? Should Marquis have to be expelled or jailed for breaking a very serious rule, even though he had acted to support a greater moral good?

Further Reflections

School life, a microcosm of the larger society, must be governed by rules of fairness that moderate student behavior and help ensure that all students will be treated as equals. But school life, concurrently, must be governed with care to ensure that students are treated fairly on an individual basis and within the context of their social relations. Care and empathy for the realities of students' lives, that is, must always temper these rules. None of us lives in a social vacuum, and in the United States the life experiences of people vary greatly across racial, cultural, and economic lines. These differences not only should be addressed in the academic curriculum, but also must be considered in the moral curriculum. Unless teachers address these differences, they cannot serve as positive models of how to make just and caring decisions.

Equally importantly, the consequence of any action must be empowering and enlightening for the parties involved. They must perceive the outcome as fair and appropriate. To do so means implementing a judicial process in which students' actions are considered in the appropriate context, intent is weighed in relation to the offense, and both students and teachers are active participants in the process. This type of action by the school system can show that despite differences in power, economics, social standing, race, or any other condition, people can be treated as of equal worth. It requires an extra measure of care if treatment is to be genuinely fair for children who ordinarily experience life as unjust.

We believe that schools and teachers must always blend the ethics of care and justice if they truly seek to meet the developmental needs of their students. This is particularly relevant for children whose lives are often devoid of acts of true kindness, justice, and fairness on the part of institutions because of their race, prior experience, or social standing. Undeniably, upholding rules is generally necessary. But, also undeniably, the school experience must not be dictated by a misguided need to maintain ideological imperatives that do not serve the needs of students. The ethics of justice and care should not function as polar extremes within the context of schools.

Primary Values and Developing Virtues of African American Ethics

John R. Snarey and Vanessa Siddle Walker

> God has two outstretched arms. One is strong enough to surround us with justice, and one is gentle enough to embrace us with grace.
> —Martin Luther King Jr., *Strength to Love*

WE BEGAN this volume with an epigraph from Carol Gilligan (1998) in which she tells the story of a seminar at which Larry Kohlberg was asked by Charles and Ronnie Blakeney, a biracial couple who were then graduate students of Kohlberg and Gilligan, "What if Heinz were Black? What would the judge do then? Wouldn't the story change? Wouldn't the conversation with the judge be different?" (p. 129). As Gilligan recalls, "We all knew that it would."

The Blakeneys' courageous voices of healthy opposition raised additional questions for all of us, questions that were reminiscent of Carol Gilligan's own broadening of the field. For example, some of Kohlberg's former students worked for years with his standard moral dilemmas, such as the one in which a man named Heinz is faced with the dilemma of stealing a drug to save his wife's life, and then these same students, all of a sudden, heard the gender bias. What was once inaudible became now strikingly easy to hear. At the point of the Blakeneys' query, the same reluctance to hearing cultural and racial differences existed. It will not be overcome until the truth is so thunderous that we can no longer avoid hearing it.

HEARING THE TWO-NESS

Unlike the either-or construction of care and justice that has polarized the moral education debate, for many in the African American community, justice and care are equally yoked and, in effect, form a unified and overarching care-and-justice ethic. An African American ethic seeks both care-fullness and fair-ness, both hand-in-handedness and even-handedness. The result is a distinctive constellation of basic values, a different moral voice, which steers the thoughts, feelings, and actions of many African Americans.

As each of the chapters in this volume reveals, African American ethics allows care-and-justice to stand in a collaborative relationship by using several ethical tools, which we have called "dual basic values." The chapters were written independently. From them, and informed by our broader training in African American history (Vanessa) and cultural differences in moral voice (John), we discerned the five justice-and-care dual values outlined in the introduction. These basic values (i.e., race-gender, resistance-accommodation, religion-ethics, agency-legacy, and community-individual) are the practical means by which justice and care work together. Some of the chapters raise or address additional African American values, of course, but we have focused on what might be called the "big five" primary dual values of an African American ethical matrix, since each was addressed to some degree by every chapter (see appendix B for a summary). The primary values, pictured as an interactive matrix, are summarized in Figure 6, along with their corresponding virtues, which will be described later in this chapter

TOWARD A CERTAIN MATURITY

Looking at Figure 6, some readers may wonder if we have abandoned a developmental approach to moral formation. The various chapters, as well, appear to give relatively little attention to developmental stages. We too, in fact, began to make this assumption until we realized that African American basic values, although they do not follow a hierarchical sequence of stages, are still clearly developmental. They move, that is, toward greater maturity.

Two simple observations can illustrate the values' developmental nature. First, there are important, if often subtle, moral-voice variations among individual African Americans. Some persons, for instance, stress resistance more than accommodation, and vice versa. Second, the

FIGURE 6. Matrix of Care and Justice Primary Values: Five Developing Virtues

	Gender[a]	Accommodation[a]	Ethics[b]	Legacy[a]	Individual[b]
Community[a]					Community + Individual: *Uplift*
Agency[b]				Agency + Legacy: *Empowerment*	
Religion[a]			Religion + Ethics: *Hope*		
Resistance[b]		Resistance + Accommodation: *Pluralism*			
Race[b]	Race + Gender: *Liberation*				

[a] Care theme, primarily

[b] Justice theme, primarily

African American community equally values both dimensions of the dual basic values but still evaluates some of these variations in moral voice as being unusually mature. Thus, some individual African Americans are regarded by the larger community as being especially "wise folk" or even "saintly" (see chapter 3). The community assumes that moral formation progresses toward a certain maturity. Now the question arises, "By what criteria are such indigenous judgments made?" Our thesis is that they are made primarily on the basis of the strength of (1) the psychological connections between, and (2) the specific *virtues* that arise out of, a mature bond between each side of a dual primary value.

Just as when one evenhandedly blends the colors blue and yellow and creates a new color, when one optimally balances the dual tones of a primary value, a new virtue emerges. By *virtue*, we mean an ethical attitude that becomes a new strength at the center of an individual's personality or character. Unusually mature African Americans attain the virtues associated with each of the dual basic values. And by virtue of these strengths, their community typically recognizes them as wise folk or leaders. The strengths are less evident, although not completely absent, among persons who have not attained such a mature, interactive balance.

The inherently social nature of such mature balancing is also seen when several persons within, say, an African American educational or religious community, come to embody these virtues and the community itself comes to be regarded by others as a "mature student body," a "mature vocal faculty," or a "mature activist congregation." We will discuss in the following sections the virtues that potentially arise from each of the dual-natured primary values (see Figure 6).

Race-and-Gender: Liberation

A primary value of African American care-and-justice ethics relates to race and gender. Race is not subordinate to gender; rather, the two are highly intertwined, just as racism and sexism in our society are highly entangled. Similarly, as Cannon (1988) and Erskine (1994) remind us, the "beloved community" of Africans in the United States is not constituted of men only or of women only; rather, it is composed of both Black men and women (cf. V. Harding, 1981, 1990). The common bond between women and the common bond between men, that is, do not take precedence over the common bond based on race. Rather, the bonds are held in interactive balance as African Americans confront the intertwined effects of gender bias and racial stereotyping.

The successful realization of a relatively balanced race-and-gender dual primary value gives rise to the virtue of *liberation*—a sense of being set free from interlocking race and gender stereotypes about what one, as a person and as a people, can and cannot do. In contrast, the weakness that arises from a notable imbalance is either *gender chauvinism*, being captive to culturally defined gender differences, as in the assumption that only men can be school principals or church pastors; or *racial prejudice*, being held a prisoner to the dominant culture's self-serving race stereotypes, as in the assumption that only Whites can become great CEOs, and only Blacks can become great tap dancers. The problem is not with either profession, of course, but rather it is being unable to escape being imprisoned by the limited options (cf. Brown, 1998, pp. 78–88; hooks, 1994, p. 112).

Liberation triumphs over potential limitations by holding together the components of race-and-gender and by speaking the truth— one can escape, one can be free, and one can help others also to realize liberation. Liberation overcomes, that is, by fostering an image of one's self as being political in the sense of being a liberator, whether one is a liberation educator, a liberation theologian, or a liberation

writer of children's books (see chapter 1). Such a liberated person regards justice as an inherent element in the care of those who are oppressed and regards caring for the defenseless as an inherent element
in creating a more just society.

Resistance-and-Accommodation: Pluralism

In the midst of oppressive circumstances, African Americans as individuals and as members of a community have embraced the basic
value of resistance-and-accommodation. Pragmatically, concurrently
opposing and accommodating the dominant society made advances
possible without jeopardizing survival. Paradoxically, it also fostered
a high degree of mutual role taking as Blacks both resisted White in-
fringements and recognized that Whites had their own interests and
thus could be worked with or manipulated as the circumstances required. This second basic value conveys great survival value and is a
cornerstone of an African American care-and-justice ethic.

The successful realization of a balanced ratio of resistance-and-
accommodation can give rise to the ethical strength of *pluralism*—initially an understanding of others, which can lead to an attitude of
respect, not just toleration, of diversity. Pluralism cherishes the ability of each cultural group to retain its unique way of life and for its
members to concurrently participate as one among equals in the life
of the larger society. In contrast, the weakness that results from a
significant imbalance is either *exclusivity*, the product of ethnocentric
resistance to accepting that all persons and peoples equally stand
within the moral sphere; or *alienation*, a sense of having made so
many accommodations that one no longer recognizes who one is or
who one's people are (Olinga, 1981; Smith, 1994; Malcolm X, 1970).

Pluralism overcomes unbalanced resistance or accommodation by
affirming that each person and community offers a certain unique in-
sight, based on the unique position in which he or she stands (see
chapter 2). The power of pluralism is evident, for instance, in the dialogues that characterize effective moral education. This type of pluralistic conversation—dialogue, can be distinguished from the more common variety of conversation—argument. Most often, arguments claim
to have answers; dialogues begin with questions. Argument aims to
end the conversation, while dialogue aims to open the conversation.
Pluralism is the virtue that allows educators to connect with others
who are different from them so that the likelihood of fair and caring
relations within schools and communities is increased (e.g., Obidah
& Teel, 2001).

Religion-and-Ethics: Hope

The central primary value of an African American care-and-justice ethical matrix is that religion is not subordinate to ethics. Rather, religious beliefs and practices are intertwined with ethics. African Americans have typically understood that religion allows one to maintain hope in the face of a world that is largely uncaring and unjust. The life histories of both communities and individuals illustrate how religion can provide people with a vision of what *ought* to be in the precarious face of what *is*. Justice and care will prevail, because history, ultimately, is in the hands of a just and caring God. African American congregations envision a God who is powerfully just and never quits caring.

The person who realizes a balanced interaction of religion-and-ethics also achieves the virtue associated with this dual basic value— *hope*—a deep attitude of confidence and trust in the belief that, ultimately, ideals and realistic expectations will become one. In its keystone role, hope also holds together the other four primary dual values and accompanying virtues of an African American ethical matrix. The weakness that can result from an unbalanced ratio of religion-and-ethics is either *ultimate despair*, a complete loss of hope in God's care and justice and, thus, a complete lack of hope for the future, or *ethical despair*, a sense that the shortcomings of current conditions, and perhaps the human condition in general, are unchangeable because all human remedies will eventually and inevitably break down and fail (cf. Williams & Williams-Morris, 2002).

Hope defeats ultimate and ethical despair by replacing them with ethical and religious assurance. Hope, in fact, was the key virtue of the civil rights movement. On one side of the movement was resistance-and-accommodation, as seen in nonviolent resistance. On the other side of the movement was agency-and-legacy, as seen in the assertion of Black power and social action. But at the center of the movement was hope—spawned by the ethical anger of a call for reform and by the religious rightness of the call for deliverance (see chapter 3).

Agency-and-Legacy: Empowerment

Often, researchers have found that oppressed peoples attribute failure or success to luck or fate rather than to their own ability or effort. Despite environmental pressure, African American ethics affirms Black agency, including social activism and interpersonal acts of kindness, in the face of a legacy of oppression. What has been handed down by a history of slavery and oppression cannot be denied, but it also must not dominate. This dual basic value nurtures African American children's sense of mutual self-and-communal resilience, responsibility, and reliance—characteristics necessary to the success of Black children operating within the reality of a mixed legacy.

The successful realization of an intensified, balanced ratio of agency-and-legacy gives rise to the ethical strength of *empowerment*—an attitude of being authorized to exert muscle and social activism on behalf of personal liberties and civil rights. Empowerment allows African Americans to tune out racist noise and provide care-and-justice for themselves and their community. In contrast, the weakness that can result from a large imbalanced ratio of agency-and-legacy is either *verbal aggression*, a form of destructive verbalization that that creates intimidation and fear among others, including teachers; or *paralyzing silence*, a form of self-destructive inaction through which the history of slavery and the continuity of racism overwhelm and silence individuals, including students (cf. Irvine, 2002; Woldemikael, 1987).

Empowerment overcomes the extremes associated with a lack of balanced agency-and-legacy precisely through its balance of speaking and acting assertively—authority with control. Empowerment thus becomes a tool for constructive change (see chapter 5). On one hand, empowerment includes the prerogative to critique the status quo. On the other hand, the empathy sponsored by a painful legacy allows one to claim the agency to change the world for the better rather than desiring to simply reverse history and oppress the oppressor.

Community-and-Individual: Uplift

The fifth basic value of African American care-and-justice is a particular understanding of community and individuality. In African American ethics, the community is not subordinate to the individual, and vice versa. To care for the group is to care for the self, and to care for the self is to care for the group. This idea is deeply embedded in West African values and was perhaps the first African American dual primary value that was identified (Herskovits, 1966). It persisted among African Americans because it greatly contributed to the ability to adapt to life under slavery and segregation.

The successful realization of a balanced community-and-individual ethic produces the fruit of *uplift*—the enhancement of the community and the valuing of the individual's diverse gifts. Through collective responsibility for the individual and individual responsibilities to the community, cycles of uplift are created. Thus, when African American teachers care for the well-being and protect the rights of an individual child, they also see themselves as providing uplift to both themselves and to the race. Individual success is inextricably linked to the uplift of the community and vice versa. In contrast, the weakness that would result from a large imbalance is either *one-sided selfishness*, acting according to one's own needs and interests without any balanced regard for the larger community; or *one-sided self-sacrifice*, the obliteration or denial of one's own interests, needs, or selfhood for the sake of "more worthy" community or cause (cf. Thurman, 1971, pp. 76–104; Smith, 1991, pp. 178–179).

Through mutual support, uplift overcomes the extremes associated with a poorly balanced community-and-individual basic value. An individual Black American's life chances are improved with the advancement of the race as a whole. The Black American community's life chances are also linked to the personal achievements of individuals. Thus, the Black community celebrates individual success. The resulting attitude of uplift is inherently ethical. "Any law that uplifts human personality is just. Any law that degrades human personality is unjust" (King, 1963b, p. 82). Any law that conveys uplift to the least advantaged among us is care-full. Any law that jeopardizes their uplift is care-less. Thus, like Mr. Dillard (chapter 4) and Ms. Jones (chapter 6), the African American tradition dismisses an individual-*versus*-community dichotomy as false, arguing that such a split between the self and the group is pragmatically dysfunctional.

Developmental Matrix, Revisited

We used the metaphor of combining two primary colors to create a new color to describe the emergence of a new virtue that develops out of the strengthened connection between and mature balancing of dual primary values. Now we must acknowledge that it is even more complicated. Mature African American moral leaders not only have full use of each set of primary values, they also know how and when to *intentionally* stress one side or the other, just as artists can combine blue and yellow to create not only a basic green, but also emerald, jade, lime, olive, and sea green. Similarly, they can create shades of hope—liberating hope, pluralistic hope, empowering hope, uplifting hope (see Figure 7).

They are able to do this because the basic values and correlated virtues have, for them, become conceptual "tools," the cognitive-neu-

FIGURE 7. Matrix of Care and Justice Primary Values: Twenty-Five Shades of Virtue

	Gender	Accommodation	Ethics	Legacy	Individual
Race	*Liberation*	Liberating Pluralism	Liberating Hope	Liberating Empowerment	Librating Uplift
Resistance	Pluralistic Liberation	*Pluralism*	Pluralistic Hope	Pluralistic Empowerment	Pluralistic Uplift
Religion	Hopeful Liberation	Hopeful Pluralism	*Hope*	Hopeful Empowerment	Hopeful Uplift
Agency	Empowering Liberation	Empowering Pluralism	Empowering Hope	*Empowerment*	Empowering Uplift
Community	Uplifting Liberation	Uplifting Pluralism	Uplifting Hope	Uplifting Empowerment	*Uplift*

ral equivalents of a painter's brushes and palette knives. They are able to use these tools, at will, to highlight ethical issues, resolve moral dilemmas, and construct effective approaches to moral education. Toward these ends, they are not afraid to take courageous stands, which may jeopardize their popularity or even their lives. In this way, they contribute to the creation of a larger social balance that better serves the common good.

SIX MORAL EXEMPLARS

Care-and-justice ethics is a developmental phenomenon, but development can be defined by mature balance and emerging virtues, not necessarily by stage and not simply by age. Thus, the manner in which African American ethics involves the collaboration of care-and-justice can be seen among both precocious schoolchildren and consummate adult educators. We will consider the ways in which six "cases," one from each chapter, embodies an African American care-and-justice ethic and, for the sake of brevity, one of the primary ways in which he or she uses a particular dual primary value and embodies its resulting virtue.

Childhood Exemplars

The three chapters in part 1 focus on moral development. From them, we chose three children: Cassie, Kwesi, and Ruby.

Cassie. Only 8 years old and in the third grade, yet Cassie Louise Lightfoot, the child's-eye narrator and star of *Tar Beach* (Ringgold, 1991), takes flight from her tar-beach rooftop in Harlem (chapter 1). In her mind's eye, she flies over the George Washington Bridge and claims it for her own. Cassie also seeks justice-and-care when she flies over the local Union Building and claims it as a gift for her father. Her dad, a working-class man nicknamed "the Cat" because of his agility when constructing bridges and multistory buildings, had helped to erect the building that now housed the local union. But he could not join it, because, during the time of Cassie's childhood, it still did not accept African Americans or Native Americans as members.

Cassie's balanced basic value of race-and-gender is evident in the attention given to race and her support of her father. As she said, her grandfather and father were not "allowed in the Union because he was colored or a half-breed Indian, like they say" (p. 26). Her biracial color vision and understanding of the basic value of *race-and-gender* gives rise to the emerging virtue of *liberation*, "for it is Cassie who has the power to emancipate her father" (p. 26). Cassie is based on Faith Ringgold's childhood memories (Ringgold, 1995). And while the virtue of liberation is unusually evident in young Cassie's personality, the adult Ringgold's life bears the mature fruit of liberation. In her words, "I am inspired by people who rise above their adversity. That's my deepest inspiration. And also I am inspired by the fact that if I really, really want to, I think I can do anything" (Ringgold, Freeman, & Roucher, 1996, p. 3). Her colortalk—in the form of story quilts, paintings, and children's books—liberates children and adults alike. In contrast to a colorblind approach, which is both uncaring (e.g., because it suppresses identities) and unjust (e.g., because it maintains social inequalities), Ringgold, through Cassie, interweaves awareness of care and justice.

Kwesi. A 17-year-old male high school senior, Kwesi is enrolled in his school's college preparatory track (chapter 2). Like his carpenter father, he loves to construct. But while his father builds the world we live in, Kwesi builds ethical values that he as an African American can live by and, thereby, resist the dominant culture. And like his mother, a nurse, he does so with great care and fairness. A conjoined ethic of care-and-justice is evident throughout Kwesi's youthful life story—caring for a White child who had fallen from her tricycle, at the heightened risk, as a Black male, of being blamed for her injury; caring for his classmates who had little religious agency and were poorly informed about the historical legacy of Christianity, at the risk of offending peers and the school's staff; demanding a truthful analysis of the way public schools function and a fair account of historical events, at the risk of being deemed a troublemaker for unveiling alternative interpretations.

Kwesi most frequently makes use of the basic value of *resistance-and-accommodation*, which has given birth to his precocious *pluralism*, as evidenced in his open-minded religiosity and his respect for individual particularity. Kwesi resists being called American, because he "never asked to be brought over here," and he resists being called Black because Whites misuse the term. Thus, he identifies himself as African. Kwesi is also willing to be called Black, however, as the situation and surroundings require, and he actually exercises an extraordinary amount of discretion and accommodation. Without one's being aware of his use of the dual basic value of resistance-and-accommodation, it would be difficult to understand the moral meaning of Kwesi's behavior, or "misbehavior."

Ruby. When only 6 years old and beginning the first grade, Ruby, for many months, faced a daily gauntlet of angry, obscenity-spewing White parents (chapter 3). They were determined that Ruby, the first Black child to desegregate New Orleans's all-White schools, would also be the last. At home, Ruby had listened to her parents debate the pros and cons of the desegregation moral dilemma they faced as a family. She heard her father's gentle voice of care and her mother's determined voice of justice (Bridges, 1999, p. 12). However, one cannot help but be struck by Ruby's own voice of moral courage, a voice beyond her years.

Ruby was carefully interviewed at the time (Coles, 1964) and also published her own retrospective account of these years (Bridges, 1999). From these sources, we know that her lived values, to varying degrees, drew from the full matrix of care-and-justice basic values, including race-and-gender: liberation (Coles, 1964, p. 51; Bridges, 1999, p. 59); resistance-and-accommodation: pluralism (Coles, 1995); agency-and-legacy: empowerment (Coles, 1986); and community-and-individual: uplift (Coles, 1964, p. 76; Bridges, 1999, pp. 38–39). Like Green (chapter 3), however, we will focus on Ruby's exemplary use of the primary dual value of religion-and-ethics simply because it is the least understood and the most hopeful.

Young Ruby came to embody the wisdom of older African American women. She did so, suggests Green (chapter 3), by absorbing and listening to "womanist" voices, which echo and extract the *religion-and-ethics* basic value from her roots in Africa and life in African American churches. Regardless of its origin, Ruby's religion-and-ethics basic value powerfully oriented her worldview (cf. Bridges, 1999, pp. 9, 48, 56, 60; Coles, 1995). The most miraculous example is that every morning on her way to school, she prayed for the mob of people who were waiting to scare her from entering the school: "Please, God, try to forgive those people. Because even if they say bad things, they don't know what they are doing. So You forgive them, just like You did those folks a long time ago when they said terrible things about you" (Bridges quoted in Coles, 1995, pp. 22–23). Each day, Ruby repeated this prayer after school as well. The virtue of *hope*, which emerged from her balance of religion-and-ethics, is what kept her going (Bridges, 1999, p. 46). Ruby, in essence, recaptured the original meaning of *womanism*.

Adulthood Exemplars

There is both continuity and discontinuity in the moral voices of children and adults. The three chapters in part 2 focused on moral education. From them, we chose three educators: Dr. Cadray, Ms. Jones, and Mr. Dillard.

Dr. Cadray. The "interventionist" described in chapter 5 was Dr. Joseph Cadray, who implemented the original educational intervention. Cadray acted as an agent of moral change by introducing a deeper understanding of care-and-justice. He did this by bringing morally problematic situations to a group of teacher educators, who responded by working through their own defensiveness and built new collective and individual understandings as a result. In ways that may not be immediately obvious, Cadray's intervention shows that justice and caring function best when they exist collaboratively. Cadray's thoughtful demonstration of the implementation of justice, without attention to caring, is a sobering description of what happens when one dimension of moral development is attended to without commitment to maintaining the other. When desegregation was pursued in a one-sided approach that aimed at justice while ignoring care, both justice and care were lost.

Cadray, in particular, employed and strengthened the basic value of moral *agency-and-legacy* among a new generation of teacher educators. Cadray, that is, knew the value of agency-and-legacy when he campaigned for the restructuring of teacher education programs and schools to enrich themselves with African American traditions and to *empower* African American students and educators by giving their traditions the same consideration as European American educational traditions. Welcoming African American traditional values as a contribution to a pluralistic foundation for restructuring urban schools can lead to more just and caring learning communities for all children. As St. John and Cadray stated, "Soliciting the voices of African American women and men to enter the center of the moral education conversation results in a restructuring of the conversation itself. . . . A new vision is needed of urban teacher education programs, in particular, one that views the African American education tradition as integral to the educational foundations of urban schools." Evidence showed that these teacher educators reframed their assumptions about teacher education and the role of the classroom teacher, making this intervention agentic.

Ms. Jones. A middle school teacher in her 6th year of teaching, Ms. Jones was Marquis's American literature teacher (chapter 6). She approached Marquis's gun dilemma with a mature grasp of care-and-justice and how this balanced ethic calls for more complex solutions to educational dilemmas than those provided by either care or justice alone. She examined the dilemma, for instance, from the perspectives of all involved—both individuals and communities. She understood the need to provide care-and-fairness for Marquis, but also for his parents, the other students, her colleagues, and herself in terms of her teaching effectiveness and career. Jones's experience further demonstrated the difficulties that occur when shortsighted policies focus on one concept without the others.

As a moral educator, Jones particularly demonstrated the dual basic value of *community-and-individual*. Ms. Jones was confronted with the expectation of the school that justice for the whole will generate care for the individual. However, as many teachers discover, she knew the premise was a fallacy. To seek just ways of handling community violence and protecting students, without concurrently expressing care for the individual nature of student needs, functions to inhibit the emerging virtue of *uplift*. When Jones upheld the "lifting as we climb" model of individual survival and success, she was uplifting the whole group and upholding an Afrocentric model of care-and-justice.

Mr. Dillard. As the principled principal of an African American school in the segregated South from 1930 to 1969, the endurance of N. Longworth Dillard (chapter 4) was the result in large part of his leadership being centered on *care-and-justice*. He saw care as a means of achieving justice and fairness as a means of achieving care. Dillard used his regular chapel talks for many purposes but chief among them was to exercise his role as a moral educator. He believed that the students needed moral instruction, so he created messages that communicated his belief about what kind of adults the children should grow up to be. The moral tone of Dillard's chapel talks is preserved in a yearbook address to the seniors. He began by quoting Horace Greeley: "Fame is vapor; popularity is an accident; riches take wings; those who cheer today will curse tomorrow; only one thing endures—character!" Dillard, in the style of a seasoned Black preacher, then elaborated on this passage.

Given that each of the five basic values are illustrated by one of the previous five moral exemplars, we will use Dillard's mature life's work to briefly show how one person embodies, to varying degrees, the full matrix of dual values and emerging character virtues. The basic value of *race-and-gender* is, no doubt, the most difficult to identify in Dillard's life because, in his segregated world, all of his students were Black and most of his staff were Black women. This much we can say, however: Through education he aimed to advance the *liberation* of both young Black women and men.

Much clearer is how Dillard embodied *resistance-and-accommodation*. For example, he argued regarding accreditation regulations, "We follow the rules until we can figure out how to change them." The resulting virtue of *pluralism* was evident in Dillard's interactional style of mingling with members of the community in informal settings and making them feel comfortable by adopting their mode of accepted communications instead of expecting them to conform to his patterns of speech. When there were disagreements, he believed in listening to people. As he said, "Let them get what they have to say off their chest. And then you reach an accommodation".

Dillard promoted an experiential, everyday-life connection of *religion-and-ethics*. He understood that the deeply embedded inequalities of the United States compelled African Americans to seek and embrace God as a just deliverer who cares for the oppressed. African

Americans had experienced the holocaust of slavery and other forms of prolonged injustice and could not interpret God from the point of privilege. Dillard did not ignore this contextual difference in orientation toward religion, for to do so would be to undermine the critical virtue of *hope* that sustains African American educational reform.

His embodiment of *agency-and-legacy* is also vividly evident as he deliberately claimed fairness and steadfastly resisted the larger, unjust system's aim of continuing to thwart the efforts of African American educators. The school he led, in fact, is an example of what African American teachers, students, and parents were able to create in spite of the inequalities they faced. Consequently, Dillard's teachers and students felt *empowered.*

Dillard cared for and treated fairly the individual student and teacher, and the student body and teaching staff collectively. His ability to balance *community-and-individual* care-and-justice within his segregated school is the most obvious of his many strengths and it may, in fact, be his most enduring legacy. He believed that he and his teachers could lift up individual students and, thereby, the race as a whole.

By balancing care and justice in their schools and in their lives, Cassie, Kwesi, Ruby, Dr. Cadray, Ms. Jones, and Mr. Dillard exemplified the broad matrix of African American exemplary virtues. In today's world, we are sometimes uncomfortable with talk of moral exemplars. Nevertheless, we all know individuals who clearly function on a broader justice-and-care playing field than ourselves. Almost invariably, these same people are examples of the primary values of religion-and-ethics (hope), resistance-and-accommodation (pluralism), agency-and-legacy (empowerment), race-and-gender (liberation), and community-and-individual (uplift). This ethical matrix also exemplifies an African American conception of moral maturity.

CONCLUSION: EDUCATION INFORMED BY AFRICAN AMERICAN VALUES PROMOTES A CERTAIN MATURITY

New strengths arise when care-and-justice basic values are one in collaboration. Educators who understand that unusual maturity is possible when the two function collaboratively maintain conversations with their students that help them to avoid dividing any of the two-storied basic values against themselves. Colorblind care and context-blind justice, in contrast, undercut care-and-justice. Teachers who seek to be caring, but refuse to care in a culturally appropriate way, are still unfair. Likewise, teachers who seek to do justice, without attention to caring for the individual, are still hurtful. Overall, as the best teachers discover, fairness and carefullness are each empty without the other. Particularly in education, a student's growth in moral balance is increasingly likely when the two function collaboratively.

If Kohlberg can be understood as creating the first major paradigm (justice) in the field of moral psychology and Gilligan can be understood as creating the second major paradigm (care) in the field, African Americans have brought to our attention the equivalent of a *third paradigm*, for the interweaving of the two represents something new. More specifically, African American ethics offers up a "big five" constellation of care-and-justice basic values and, developing from their optimal balance, five correlated virtues: gender-race (liberation), resistance-accommodation (pluralism), religion-ethics (hope), agency-legacy (power), and community-individual (uplift). These conjunctive care-and-justice values, of course, invite further analysis and future research.

Our Final Word

This volume has not, of course, argued that African Americans have a monopoly on this third paradigm or are the only group to have experienced racial injustice (cf. Angelou, 1993). Our nation has much to learn from, and stands to be enriched by, a broad spectrum of different racial-ethnic voices. Nevertheless, even a genuinely sympathetic reader may feel compelled to protest, "African Americans are not the only people who hold these values!" A legacy of our nation's history of racism, unfortunately, is not only the holocaust of slavery but also the reflexive desire of many Anglo-Americans to feel superior to, rather than to learn from, African Americans.

The justice-and-care matrix emerged out of a constructive enterprise. This model is a conceptual tool, not a reified entity, for thinking about moral formation and designing multicultural moral education. No doubt, other tools and models are possible. We invite the reader to fashion and bring new tools to the table. Notwithstanding this inevitable limitation, our hope is that this book's collective voices open up the conversation and push the field to a more thoughtful, racially inclusive approach to moral formation. This includes not only moral education but also moral-education research. Importantly, as both Duncan and Green emphasized, for Black moral perspectives to be accurately represented in the research literature, researchers must

first confront issues of injustice and carelessness in the way they conduct empirical studies that engage or exclude the moral viewpoints of
African Americans.

The plea of *Race-ing Moral Formation* has been that we open our
ears to the moral voices of African Americans and, in this process of
moral formation, come to realize that no single voice is ever adequate,
so a plurality of tongues is essential. No one ethnic-racial group hears
the whole truth nor only the truth, but African Americans do acquire
a partial superiority of hearing and understanding from the particular
place in which they sit at the world's table. The imaginative listening
to, caring for, and honoring African American voices are critical components of moral education and moral maturity. For this we hope, for
this is care-and-justice.

Epilogue

Charles D. Blakeney and Ronnie Frankel Blakeney

> I speak of the black experience, but I am always talking to the human condition.
> —Maya Angelou, *Discovering Authors*

WRITING THE epilogue for this book, and considering the issues it raises, is like standing on a mountaintop. One can look back, hear echoes, and look forward to see the way in which the African American experience continues to forge justice and care into an integrating moral matrix. We recall the responses of more than 200 African Americans who responded almost 30 years ago when we asked, "What if Heinz were Black?" We hear the echoes of those voices in the courageous and caring essays in this collection as they bring both color and colorblindness out of the closet.

ECHO FROM THE PAST

What we heard, and hear now in *Race-ing Moral Formation*, was not what we expected. As educators and researchers, we were struggling to balance the universal (theory) and the particular (situated experience). We reasoned that being a member of a historically oppressed minority group meant that identity (particularly group identity) would be constructed around the core issues of justice. The "Self" would be defined in opposition to the antagonistic "Unjust Other." We postulated a theory of moral discordance wherein minority status identity would inform moral voice, moral choice, and the structure of moral

147

reasoning such that we would hear discordant voices when race was introduced into the context of a moral dilemma. We bravely, and in hindsight naively, held fast to a justice hypothesis and assumed it to be universal. We asked African American adults, adolescents, and children, "What if two children were drowning, and you could save only one. One is Black and the other is not. What should you do?"

We learned that both an unequal distribution of power *and* cultural affinity affect inter-group relations. Fully one-third of the participants in our study gave answers that conformed to our justice hypothesis. "I don't think of myself as prejudiced," a young woman told us, "but I have to figure that nine out of the next ten people who walk by will be White, and more than likely they will be racist. So I have some kind of obligation to save the Black one." Two-thirds of the subjects, however, did not support the hypothesis.

One third defined themselves as Black within the context of culture and history. For members of this group, moral choice often varied by racial context, which they usually justified as an extension of kinship concern. "It's like the difference between running over a jack rabbit, and running over a rabbit that you raised in the backyard," a young man told us. The last third of the group had no sense of themselves as members of an oppressed minority group, nor did racial context impinge on moral judgment. "I'll save whoever's closer. Then she'll be my friend and play with me," a preteen responded. By listening, we learned the power of people to tell their own truth, despite our hypotheses.

We were blessed to have teachers, including Larry Kohlberg and Carol Gilligan, who weren't threatened when we asked questions about race. Instead, they encouraged us. "Good question!" they said. "Bring us some data." In *Race-ing Moral Formation* we have both good questions and challenging data.

VISION FOR THE FUTURE

What are the questions that this collection raises for the practice of moral education, as well as for the future of international and race relations? How do we understand the interweaving of ethnic and diasporic identities in the course of individual and societal development? Are Black adolescent voices of resistance (see chapter 2) and Black women's integration of race and gender (see chapter 3) universal adaptive postures writ bold in African American communities? What can we learn about educational practice, policy, and teacher preparation for the complicated real world from the exposition of the three ways that "Ms. Jones" might handle a clinical moral dilemma in an urban classroom (see chapter 6)? How should we value colortalk and colorblindness (e.g., chapter 1) for the future? These are not comfortable questions. If we are looking for pat answers, we don't find them here.

Garrett Duncan (chapter 2) and Andrea Green (chapter 3) each describe a moral perspective that represents something "other than" the perspectives of justice and care offered by Kohlberg and Gilligan. Duncan presents three forms of diasporic identity. These are ways that Black youth resist the dominant paradigm to "Honor the integrity of their primary cultural identity," work toward social-moral transformation, and thus negotiate biculturalism. Andrea Green also describes a necessary resistance to the "mirror" held up to Black women by the larger, Euro-American society, which, in Du Bois' words "looks on in amused contempt and pity." Green outlines, instead, womanist values, derived from the community of African American women. The values of improvisation, unction, suspicion of assimilation, interconnectedness, and spirituality allow African American women (and others who find themselves similarly situated) to construct and negotiate resistant ways to know "who we are" and "whose we are." Are resistance and belonging universal moral strivings?

Audrey Thompson (chapter 1) and Vanessa Siddle Walker and Renarta Tompkins (chapter 4) suggest that acknowledging race and racism provides the platform for a community of care to fight against injustice. Thompson shows us that "colorblind racial etiquette" is a new, liberal racism that denies the lived experience of prejudice and discrimination that is shared in the African American community. Does speaking aloud about the "American family secret" take away its power to wound? Siddle Walker and Tompkins describe the focus on character, uplift, and spiritual guidance that empowered Black principals, teachers, and children in segregated schools embedded in caring communities to struggle for integrity and justice. Edward P. St. John and Joseph Cadray (chapter 4) show how an ethic of care and the practice of moral dilemma discussion can be transplanted from traditional segregated African American schools into a cross-cultural teacher-training program that bridges the mission-practice gap. This bold experiment enhanced both program effectiveness and professional integrity. These chapters raise additional provocative, testable questions: To what extent do we need caring community to sustain our efforts to struggle for justice (chapter 4)? Alternately, can a close-knit caring community be replicated without the shared experience of injustice (chapter 5)? How do we reconcile respect for the other as an individual with the recognition of group identity? Is there such a thing as "colorblind justice"? Is there something to be gained from segregated schooling? Is the cauldron of racial injustice necessary to forge moral exemplars like Ruby and Mr. Dillard? Are we made stronger as individuals, more cohesive as a group, and more truthful as a society by fighting over these issues? The questions raised by the examples in every chapter (from the dilemmas raised by children's books marred by "colorblind racial etiquette" to contemporary moral dilemmas in inner-city classrooms raised by Obidah, Jackson-Minot, Monroe, and Williams) provide a veritable treasure chest of material for classroom and community discussion, as well as for research and theory building.

Race-ing Moral Formation offers three important contributions to future conversations about moral development theory and practice. First, the individual essays themselves bring much needed contemporary African American perspectives "to the table" from a variety of settings: children's literature, middle school classrooms, women's "rooms," segregated schools, urban schools. Each essay uncovers a truth that "we all knew," but didn't want to admit in mixed company: even in this new millennium, color matters. Second, Siddle Walker and Snarey in their introductory and concluding chapters frame the essays with their "Interactive Matrix of Justice-and-Care Primary Values." This moral matrix creates a map for understanding both the interaction of justice and care in each of the dual values they outline and a guide for understanding the particular interaction of those value-duos in the African American experience. The third incalculable value of this collection, because of both its specific examples and its theoretical vision, is the contribution of a new model of moral understanding in the context of real world experiences of injustice and uncaring. The model of Siddle Walker and Snarey should take its place beside those of Frantz Fanon, Viktor Frankl, and Paolo Freire. With a cross-culturally accessible moral tone, along with resources and exercises for teachers, the authors share a model of *liberation* (rather than limitation), *pluralism* (rather than monopoly), *hope* (rather than hate), *empowerment* (rather than enslavement), and *uplift* (rather than retribution). As each of us struggle for integrity in a complicated world, *Race-ing Moral Formation* should prove useful across a range of settings, from family counseling and classroom discussion to international efforts to negotiate peace.

Guide to Suggested
Chapter-Correlated Films

Chapter 1

Ruby Bridges   (biography, 90 minutes, VHS, G)

RELEVANCE: This film is a dramatic presentation of the experiences of 6-year old Ruby Bridges, the African American girl who was the first child to integrate the New Orleans public schools in 1960. The film also documents Dr. Robert Coles's relationship with Ruby, as it conveys her remarkable child's-eye view of morality and religion, her mother's voice of justice, and her father's voice of care.

PRIMARY CHARACTERS:
Ruby Nell Bridges (Chaz Monet)
Mrs. Lucille Bridges, mother (Lela Rochon)
Mr. Avis Bridges, father (Michael Beach)
Mrs. Henry, schoolteacher (Penelope Ann Miller)
Dr. Robert (Bob) Coles, psychiatrist (Kevin Pollak)

DIRECTOR: Euzhan Palcy

DISTRIBUTOR: Disney

Chapter 2

The Fire This Time   (documentary, 90 minutes, VHS, R)

RELEVANCE: The focus of this documentary is on the factors that contributed to the 1992 racial unrest in South Central Los Angeles associated with the videotaped brutal police beating of Rodney King. The film captures the conditions that inform the diverse and conflicting "play of voices" discussed in Garrett Duncan's chapter.

PRIMARY CHARACTERS:
Los Angeles youth and adult residents
Black civic and religious social leaders (e.g., the late Betty Shabazz,
    Andrew Young, Michael Zinzun)
Black cultural and political organizations (e.g., Black Panther Party,
    Crips and Bloods gang members)

DIRECTOR: Randy Holland

DISTRIBUTOR: Rhino Home Video

Chapter 3

Beloved   (drama, 180 minutes, VHS, DVD, R)

RELEVANCE: This complex film is a faithful adaptation of Toni Morrison's Pulitzer Prize–winning novel, *Beloved*. Set in rural Cincinnati, Ohio, in 1873, it captures the legacy of slavery, and how the psyche defends itself, in part through haunting flashbacks of disturbing experiences (lynching, rape, neglect). This is a disturbing film that may not be suitable for all classrooms (rated R for nudity and violence); nevertheless, it captures the spirit and spirituality of Andrea Green's chapter.

PRIMARY CHARACTERS:
Sethe, former slave (Oprah Winfrey)
Paul D, former slave, Sethe's lover (Danny Glover)
Beloved, Sethe's third child (Thandie Newton)
Denver, Sethe's fourth and youngest child (Kimberly Elise)
Baby Suggs, former slave, preacher, and Sethe's mother-in-law (Beah
    Richards)
Younger Sethe (Lisa Gay Hamilton)
Stamp Paid, former slave (Albert Hall)
Ella, Baby Suggs's neighbor (Irma Hall)
Amy Denver, White indentured slave girl (Kessia Kordelle)
Schoolteacher, wicked widower (Jude Ciccolella)
Lady Jones, biracial neighbor of Baby Suggs (Jane White)
Edward Bodwin, Quaker abolitionist (Jason Robards, Jr.)
Here Boy (dog)

DIRECTOR: Jonathan Demme

DISTRIBUTOR: Buena Vista

Chapter 4

The Road to Brown: The Man Who Killed Jim Crow   (documentary biography, 56 minutes, VHS, NR)

RELEVANCE: This film tells the story of Charles (Charley) Hamilton Houston (1895–1950), the first Black editor of the *Harvard Law Review*, who became the and chief counsel to the National Association for the Advancement of Colored People (NAACP), and who became known as "the man who killed Jim Crow" because his legal assault on Jim Crow laws guided the nation toward the landmark *Brown vs. Board of Education* decision. Houston's work, in effect, launched the civil rights movement. In the process of telling this important story, the film also provides a concise summary of the historical context of segregated schools and the ways we have commonly understood what precipitated desegregation. Houston was a model of moral maturity, and a brief quote from him near the end of the film illustrates his use of justice reasoning.

PRIMARY CHARACTER: James Hamilton Houston

DIRECTOR: William Elwood

DISTRIBUTOR: California Newsreel

Chapter 5

Remember the Titans   (drama, 113 minutes, VHS, DVD, PG)

RELEVANCE: The film is based on the true story of desegregation in a high school in Alexandria, Virginia, in 1971. The experience of a high school football team powerfully portrays themes of care, justice, and interracial relations.

PRIMARY CHARACTERS:
Coach Herman Boone (Denzel Washington)
Coach Bill Yoast (Will Patton)
Petey Jones (Donald Faison)
Julius "Big Ju" Campbell (Wood Harris)
Gerry Bertier (Ryan Hurst)
Lewis Lastik (Ethan Suplee)
Carol Boone (Nicole Ari Parker)

Sheryl Yoast (Hayden Panettiere)
Jerry "The Rev" Harris (Craig Kirkwood)

DIRECTOR: Boaz Yakin

DISTRIBUTOR: Disney

Chapter 6

Light It Up   (drama, 99 minutes, VHS, DVD, R)

RELEVANCE: A shooting incident in an inner-city (Queens, New York)
school results in a police officer being wounded; a group of desperate
students hold the officer hostage. While more violent than Jennifer
Obidah's gun dilemma in chapter 6, it raises many of the same moral
issues and also shows a teacher building positive relationships with
students.

PRIMARY CHARACTERS:
Lester Dewitt (Usher Raymond)
Officer Dante Jackson (Forest Whitaker)
Stephanie Williams (Rosario Dawson)
Zacharias "Ziggy" Malone (Robert Ri'chard)
Ken Knowles (Judd Nelson)
Rodney J. Templeto (Fredro Starr)
Lynn Sabatini (Sara Gilbert)
Robert "Rivers" Tremont (Clifton Collins Jr.)
Principal Armstrong (Glynn E. Turman)
Captain Monroe (Vic Polizos)
Audrey McDonald (Vanessa L. Williams)

DIRECTOR: Craig Bolotin

DISTRIBUTOR: 20th Century Fox

Overview of African American Primary Values Across the Chapters

The five dual primary values were described in the introduction and their resulting virtues were described in the conclusion. This appendix highlights some of the ways that each chapter contributes to our understanding of each of the big five justice-and-care themes.

Race-and-Gender (Liberation)

Chapter 1. Thompson notes that in African American ethics it is impossible to separate ethical considerations from contextual considerations, including the gendered sociocultural system. All African Americans, both male and female, experience societal marginalization, but gender also moderates the style by which all experience the unethical repercussions of racism.

Chapter 2. Duncan observed that Black youth are quick to point out the social fabrications that serve to dehumanize them. High school girls in Duncan's study easily rejected the blond, blue-eyed, ladylike ideal offered by the larger society. Black male high school students were critical of fabricated male role models that they believed reflected the images or agendas of White society. Race and gender, that is, were interlocking discourses when it comes to the experiences of Black adolescents.

Chapter 3. Green, using womanist theory, explored the intertwined relationship of race and gender in the basic moral values of African Americans. Her womanist method revealed the norms and ideals of the African American folk community that have been inherited, retained, and developed in spite of, and in defense against, raced and gendered oppression.

Chapter 4. Siddle Walker and Tompkins observed that, historically, the voices of both men and women teaching in the African American schools of the segregated South embodied both justice and care. Simply put, male teachers were caring as well as fair; female teachers were fair as well as caring. Further, perhaps in part because of their shared oppression, African American men and women often functioned as partners in their task of racial uplift.

Chapter 5. St. John and Cadray noted that the moral-education conversation needs to be broadened to include the voices of womanists (i.e., primarily Black feminist scholars) and liberationists (i.e., primarily Black male critical theorists) in teacher- and moral-education theory and practice. Soliciting the voices of African American women and men to enter the center of the education conversations, they believe, will result in a restructuring of the educational foundations of urban schools.

Chapter 6. Obidah and her colleagues observed that, in the daily educational practices of urban schools, racial and gender discrimination are intertwined. They illustrate that an intertwined care-and-justice ethics must be implemented in order to moderate, for instance, the prevalent suspicion of Black male students.

Resistance-and-Accommodation (Pluralism)

Chapter 1. Thompson reminds us that Black educators are likely to acknowledge racism as an issue or to use colortalk to help their students to resist unjust and oppressive social relations. In Black feminist literature also, outspokenness and honest anger are crucial to trusting relations. Black feminists, further, resist treating Whiteness as the norm against which Black problems are identified and resist accepting the myth of colorblindness.

Chapter 2. Duncan, in essence, intentionally selected his study participants because they exhibited the strategic use of cultural separatism and cultural negotiation responses in their daily interactions with teachers and peers. The resistance-and-accommodation subvarieties of resistance that he identifies go against the grain of dominant institutions, but they are also forms of accommodation because they take dominant institutions seriously enough to critique them.

Chapter 3. Green presents additional unearthed images of Black women's ethics that resists blind assimilation. She identifies, for instance, a suspicion of assimilating the narratives of White culture. African

American adolescent girls, for instance, often resist or "dis"-regard dominant constructions of femininity. Green asserts that any theory of Black women's moral development must attend to the social and collective process of selecting or rejecting dominant cultural values.

Chapter 4. Siddle Walker and Tompkins remind us that African Americans normally believe in rules and fairness (and teach children to follow them, because breaking them could be deadly). Nevertheless, African Americans are often suspicious of Whites' notions of what is fair. Therefore, the authors approvingly quote Principal Dillard: "We follow the rules until we can figure out how to change them."

Chapter 5. St. John and Cadray, focusing on university teacher education and leadership programs, argued that interventions at an urban university could play a more active role by helping African American educators resist unnecessary accommodations to the status quo and also require members of the dominant group to accommodate themselves to the reasonable assimilation of rich African American traditions.

Chapter 6. Obidah and her colleagues suggest that, because Africans in America typically have lived on the periphery of mainstream White society, they were able to maintain and develop unique moral tools. Often, these tools supported their survival by wisely balancing resistance and accommodation. Black schoolchildren especially need such tools because mainstream educational institutions often fail to protect them from injustice or to provide them with adequate care.

Religion-and-Ethics (Hope)

Chapter 1. Thompson observed that an African American in Heinz's place normally would have been able to look to the church for help. African Americans' moral agency is affirmed by Black support systems, the most central of which is the Black Church. Through their religious involvement, many African American children and youth become aware that they have a voice.

Chapter 2. Duncan draws on the words of Frederick Douglass, abolitionist and critic of the practice of Christianity, to illustrate the transgressive-profane moral voice of resistance that he has identified. Duncan also noted that Douglass qualified his critique by strictly applying it to the "slave-holding, women-whipping, cradle-plundering" religion of this land, in contrast to the uplifting "Christianity of Christ." Like Douglass, Duncan was careful to hold religion and ethics in balance.

Chapter 3. Green provides the most extensive treatment of the theme of religion and ethics. She shows that African American ancestors, understood in the diasporan context as spiritual intermediaries, bequeathed to their descendants a collection of moral strategies for coping with oppressive conditions. From her womanist theological perspective, the resulting moral virtues are understood as divine gifts and, thus, "wise folk" are not only moral exemplars but also spiritual saints.

Chapter 4. Siddle Walker and Tompkins depict an undercurrent of religion that motivates the caring, fair practices of Black schools in the old South. These beliefs are expressed as individual commitments that are used to explain the behavior of the one caring and form the basis of morality within group activities. In the schools that have been studied to date, the principals' admonishments often were grounded in Christian theology.

Chapter 5. St. John and Cadray did not give much attention to the religion-ethics linkage, perhaps because they were addressing teacher education in public universities. Nevertheless, they note approvingly that in one school, which had been an African American school before desegregation, a teacher felt comfortable borrowing a church's bus to take the children on school-sponsored field trips.

Chapter 6. Obidah and her colleagues, who also focused on a public school setting, do not directly address the role of religion-and-ethics. Nevertheless, they begin their chapter with an approving reference to the colonial-era "dame" schools that included explicit ethical instruction based on Christian values.

Agency-and-Legacy (Empowerment)

Chapter 1. For Thompson, naming oppression is an act of agency. The legacy of slavery and racism must be acknowledged. African American communities juggle the possibility of agency and the legacy of racist oppression. Thompson quotes Desmond, a Black high school student, to capture this point: "When they talk about us, they talk about us being in chains. They don't talk about how we got out of it, what we did for ourselves."

Chapter 2. Duncan presents three conjunctive African voices, all of which reflect the larger basic value of agency-and-legacy. All three diasporan voices, that is, reflect the construction of moral beliefs that are explicitly associated with issues of agency and the legacy of oppression.

Chapter 3. Green provides many examples of agency exhibited by African Americans during and under the legacy of slavery. She uses the term *unction*, from African American folk culture, to demonstrate the agentic power of African American tradition. The agency to speak, she noted, became closely aligned with the power to heal the wounds of slavery and experience liberation.

Chapter 4. As Siddle Walker and Tompkins concluded, well-trained and caring teachers in the Black schools of the segregated South committed themselves to providing educational opportunities, including a strong curriculum and extracurricular activities, for the children with whom they worked. They demonstrated and reinforced the sense of agency and the belief that African Americans could overcome the legacy of slavery and be successful in a variety of arenas.

Chapter 5. The intervention described by St. John and Cadray involved posing moral dilemmas to teacher educators, which enabled them to ponder the ethical foundations for their teaching practices. Cadray acted as an agent of change by introducing a deeper understanding of the lives of African American children into the discussion among teacher educators in an urban university. His agency was conscious and intentional; he aimed to heighten awareness of the legacy of racism and to promote change.

Chapter 6. Obidah and her colleagues observed that the decision of Marquis to bring a gun to school was actually an act of moral agency in that he acted to save his father's life. The authors observed that, at Kohlberg's Stage 4, supporting families is just as essential as obeying the law to preserve an orderly society and, at Kohlberg's Stage 5, the school policy can be seen as serving a lesser value than Marquis's aim to save his father's life. Marquis's agency, that is, could be understood as mature resistance to the legacy of slavery, which had undoubtedly affected the outlook and actions of his family members.

Community-and-Individual (Uplift)

Chapter 1. Thompson sheds light on how both community and individuality are highly valued in the Black community. In essence, a sense of pluralism is promoted in which the gifts of each human being are appreciated, and his or her diversity, in turn, contributes to the resources available for the community's survival. African American individuals understand themselves as interdependent within the community and thus are often are involved in networks of community care and social activism.

Chapter 2. Duncan indicates that the conjunctive voices he identifies among African American adolescents had their origin in stories passed on to youth from their community.

Chapter 3. Green notes that positive self-images for African Americans are rooted in the webs of connection in which we live. Person-folk interconnectedness constitutes the central ingredient of the conventions of care of self and others and is the basis for a dual public ethic of Black self-reliance and community support.

Chapter 4. Siddle Walker and Tompkins note that every African American segregated school reported in the scholarly literature had some array of clubs that were maintained by the principal and teachers and financed, in part, by the African American school community. That the community supplied the funding ensured a remarkable degree of distributive justice in that all students had opportunities to participate and not simply those students with more family resources.

Chapter 5. St. John and Cadray exhibit the community-individual dual theme in their use of both traditional (person-centered) and alternative (community-centered) frames of teacher preparation. In one sense, the alternative frames represent a critique of traditional education, but in another sense, the two themes are used in a contrapuntal fashion to point to a more complex person-and-community orientation grounded in African American tradition.

Chapter 6. Obidah addresses the individual-and-community theme by focusing on one teacher's encounter with one student's moral dilemma as it was manifested within a school community. Interpersonal interconnection and community leaders' support were mobilized by Ms. Jones to protect an individual student, while concurrently there was mindfulness of the importance of law and order for maintenance of an educational community.

References

Akinyela, M. (2003). Battling the serpent: Nat Turner, Africanized Christianity, and a Black ethos. *Journal of Black Studies, 33*(3), 255–280.

Aldridge, D. P. (1999). Conceptualizing a DuBoisian philosophy of education. *Educational Theory, 49,* 359–379.

Alexander, L. (1992). Identifying Americans of African descent. *Western Journal of Black Studies, 16,* 141–146.

Alleyne Johnson, J. (1995). Life after death: Critical pedagogy in an urban classroom. *Harvard Educational Review, 65,* 213–230.

Altenbaugh, R. (1992). *The teacher's voice.* Washington, DC: Falmer Press.

Anderson, V. (1995). *Beyond ontological blackness.* New York: Continuum.

Angelou, M. (1993). "Maya Angelou." In *Discovering Authors* (CDROM). Detroit, MI: Gale Research.

Arendt, H. (1970). *On violence.* San Diego: Harvest/HBJ.

Argyris, C. (1993). *Knowledge for action.* San Francisco: Jossey-Bass.

Ashmore, H. (1954). *The Negro and the schools.* Chapel Hill: University of North Carolina Press.

Astor, R. A., Meyer, H. A., & Behre, W. J. (1999). Unowned places and times: Maps and interviews about violence in high schools. *American Educational Research Journal, 36,* 3–42.

Baldwin, J. (1993). If Black English ain't a language, then tell me what is? In D. Gioseffi (Ed.), *On prejudice* (pp. 372–375). New York: Anchor Books.

Banks, J. A. (1993). The cannon debate, knowledge construction, and multicultural education. *Educational Researcher, 22*(5), 4–14.

Banks, J. A. (2002). Race, knowledge construction and education in the USA: Lessons from history. *Race, Ethnicity & Education, 5*(1), 7–27.

Barksdale, R., & Kinnamon, K. (1972). *Black writers of America.* New York: Macmillan.

Barnes, E. (1972). The Black community as the source of positive self-concept for Black children: A theoretical perspective. In R. L. Jones (Ed.), *Black psychology* (pp. 166–193). New York: Harper & Row.

Barnwell, Y. M. (1992). No mirrors in my nana's house. Performed on the compact disc recording, *Still on the journey,* by Sweet Honey in the Rock. Washington, DC: BMI Barnwell's Notes.

Beauboeuf-Lafontant, T. (1999). A movement against and beyond boundaries:

"Politically relevant teaching" among African American teachers. *Teachers College Record, 100*, 702–723.

Belenky, M. F., Bond, L. A., & Weinstock, J. S. (1997). *A tradition that has no name.* New York: Basic Books.

Billingsley, A. (1973). Black families and White social science. In J. Ladner (Ed.), *The death of White sociology* (pp. 431–450). Baltimore: Black Classic Press.

Billingsley, A. (1992). *Climbing Jacob's ladder: The enduring legacy of African American families.* New York: Simon & Schuster.

Blakeney, R., & Blakeney, C. (1992). Growing pains: A theory of stress and moral conflict. *Counseling and Values, 36*, 162–175.

Blakeney, C., & Blakeney, R. (1996). A therapeutic just community for troubled girls. *Reclaiming Children and Youth, 5*(3), 163–172.

Blizek, W. (1999). Caring, justice, and self-knowledge. In M. Katz, N. Noddings, & K. Strike (Eds.), *Justice and caring* (pp. 93–109). New York: Teachers College Press.

Brabeck, M. E. (1989). Comment on Scarr. *American Psychologist, 89*(5), 847.

Bragg, R. (1997, December 3). Forgiveness, after 3 die in Kentucky shooting. *New York Times*, p. A.16.

Bridges, R. (1999). *Through my eyes.* New York: Scholastic.

Brown, L. M. (1998). *Raising their voices: The politics of girls' anger.* Cambridge, MA: Harvard University Press.

Brown, L. M., & Gilligan, C. (1992). *Meeting at the crossroads: Women's psychology and girls' development.* Cambridge, MA: Harvard University Press.

Brown, L. M., Tappan, M., & Gilligan, C. (1995). Listening to different voices. In W. Kurtines & J. Gewirtz (Eds.), *Moral development* (pp. 311–355). Boston: Allyn & Bacon.

Browne, I. (1999). *Latinas and African American women at work.* New York: Russell Sage Foundation.

Burke, R. W., & Nieremberg, I. (1998). In search of the inspirational in teachers and teaching. *Journal for a Just and Caring Education, 4*, 336–355.

Cadray, J. P. (1995). Enhancing multiculturalism in a teacher preparation program: A reflective analysis of a practitioner's intervention. *Dissertation Abstracts International, 57*(8), 3332.

Cadray, J. P. (1997). Deconstructing bias: Reframing the teacher preparation curriculum. *Journal for a Just and Caring Education, 3*, 76–94.

Cadray, J. P. (2001). [Review of the book *Company in your classroom*]. *Journal of Moral Education, 3*(2), 207–210.

Canada, G. (1995). *Fist, stick, knife, gun.* Boston: Beacon Press.

Cannon, K. G. (1988). *Black womanist ethics.* Atlanta: Scholars Press.

Cannon, K. G. (1995). *Katie's canon: Womanism and the soul of the Black community.* New York: Continuum.

Carroll, R. (1997). *Sugar in the raw: Voices of young Black girls in America.* New York: Crown.

Castenell, L. A., Jr., & Pinar, W. F. (Eds.) (1993). *Understanding curriculum as racial text*. Albany: State University of New York Press.

Cecelski, D. (1994). *Along freedom road: Hyde County, North Carolina, and the fate of Black schools in the South*. Chapel Hill: University of North Carolina Press.

Centers for Disease Control and Prevention. (1996, September 27). Youth risk behavior surveillance, United States, 1996. *Morbidity and Mortality Weekly Report, 45*, 32–40.

Chalmers, V. (1997). White out: Multicultural performances in a progressive school. In M. Fine, L. Weis, L. C. Powell, & L. M. Wong (Eds.), *Off White* (pp. 66–78). New York: Routledge.

Christy, K. S. (1998). *"She's from Brooklyn, you know": African American students' perceptions of White teachers' trustworthiness*. Paper presented at the annual meeting of the American Educational Studies Association, Philadelphia, PA.

Clarke, J. (1966). The boy who painted Christ black. In J. Clarke (Ed.), *American Negro short stories* (pp. 108–114). New York: Hill & Wang.

Clayton, R. W. (1990). *Mother wit: The ex-slave narratives of the Louisiana Writers' Project*. New York: Peter Lang.

Colby, A., & Kohlberg, L. (1987). *The measurement of moral judgment* (2 vols.). Cambridge, England: Cambridge University Press.

Coles, R. (1964). *Children of crisis: Vol. 1. A study of courage and fear*. Boston: Little, Brown.

Coles, R. (1986). *The moral life of children*. New York: Grove/Atlantic.

Coles, R. (1995). *The story of Ruby Bridges*. New York: Scholastic.

Collins, P. H. (1990). *Black feminist thought. Knowledge, consciousness, and the politics of empowerment*. Boston: Unwin Hyman.

Collins, P. H. (1998). *Fighting words: Black women and the search for justice*. Minneapolis: University of Minnesota Press.

Collins, P. H. (2003). Some group matters: Intersectionality, situated standpoints, and Black feminist thought. In T. Lott (Ed.), *A companion to African-American philosophy* (pp. 205–229). Malden, MA: Blackwell.

Comer, J. P., Haynes, N. M., Joyner, E. T., & Ben-Avie, M. (Eds.) (1996). *Rallying the whole village: The Comer process for reforming education*. New York: Teachers College Press.

Conrad, C. F., Brier, E. M., & Braxton, J. M. (1997). Factors contributing to matriculation of White students in public HBCUs. *Journal for a Just and Caring Education, 3*, 37–62.

Cooper, A. J. (1892). *A voice from the South, by a black woman of the South*. Xenia, OH: Aldine.

Cooper-Lewter, N., & Mitchell, H. H. (1986). *Soul theology*. Nashville, TN: Abingdon Press.

Corrigan, M. B. (1994). "It's a family affair": Buying freedom in the District of Columbia, 1850–1860. In L. E. Hudson Jr. (Ed.), *Working toward freedom* (pp. 163–191). Rochester, NY: University of Rochester Press.

Cross, B. E. (1993, May). How do we prepare teachers to improve race relations? *Educational Leadership, 50,* 64–65.

Cross, W. (1991). *Shades of black: Diversity in African-American identity.* Philadelphia: Temple University Press.

Cuban, L. (1993). *How teachers taught: Constancy and change in American classrooms, 1880–1990* (2nd ed.). New York: Teachers College Press.

Curtis, P. (1993). *Relationships between agency and social perspective coordination as perspective-taking components in Black children, aged 8–15.* Unpublished doctoral dissertation, Emory University, Atlanta, GA.

Curtis-Tweed, P. (2003). Experiences of African American empowerment. *Journal of Moral Education, 32*(4), 351–364.

Darder, A. (1991). *Culture and power in the classroom.* New York: Bergin & Garvey.

Darder, A. (1995). *Culture and difference.* New York: Bergin & Garvey.

Davidson, F. (1974). *Respect for human dignity and ethnic judgments in childhood.* Unpublished doctoral dissertation, Harvard University, Cambridge, MA.

Davidson, F., & Davidson, M. (1994). *Changing childhood prejudice: The caring work of the schools.* Westport, CT: Bergin & Garvey.

Davis, L. G. (1996). *A history of Beaufort/Queen Street High School: 1928–1968.* Kingston, NY: Tri State Services.

deAnda, D. (1984). Bicultural socialization: Factors affecting the minority experience. *Social Work, 29,* 101–107.

DeHaan, R., Hanford, R., Kinlaw, K., Philler, D., & Snarey, J. (1997). Promoting ethical reasoning, affect, and behavior among high school students. *Journal of Moral Education, 56*(1), 5–20.

Dei, G. J. S. (1994). Afrocentricity: A cornerstone of pedagogy. *Anthropology and Education Quarterly, 25*(1), 3–28.

Delpit, L. (1995). *Other people's children: Cultural conflict in the classroom.* New York: New Press.

Dempsey, V., & Noblit, G. (1993). The demise of caring in an African American community: One consequence of school desegregation. *The Urban Review, 25,* 47–61.

Dillard, N. (1942). *A survey of the extra curricular programs in five Negro secondary schools of North Carolina.* Unpublished master's thesis, University of Michigan, Ann Arbor.

Diver-Stamnes, A. C. (1995). *Lives in the balance: Youth, poverty, and education in Watts.* Albany: State University of New York Press.

Douglass, F. (1845). *Narrative of the life of Frederick Douglass, an American slave, written by himself.* Boston: The Anti-Slavery Office. (Reprinted in 1968 by the New American Library, New York.)

Du Bois, W. E. B. (1903). *The souls of Black folk.* New York: Bantam Books.

Duncan, G. (1993). Racism as a developmental mediator. *The Educational Forum, 57,* 360–370.

Duncan, G. (1996). Space, place, and the problematic of race: Black adolescent discourse as mediated action. *Journal of Negro Education, 65,* 133–150.

Duncan, G. (2000). Race and human rights violations in the United States: Considerations for human rights and moral educators. *Journal of Moral Education, 29*(2), 183–201.

Duncan, G. (2002). Critical race theory and method: Rendering race in ethnographic research. *Qualitative Inquiry, 8*(1), 83–102.

Eaker-Rich, D., & Van Galen, J. (Eds.). (1996). *Caring in an unjust world.* Albany: State University of New York Press.

Edwards, A. (1998). *Booker T. Washington High School (1916–1974): Voices of remembrance.* Paper presented at the Southern History of Education Society's annual meeting, Georgia State University, Atlanta.

Edwards, W., Royster, P., & Bates, L. (1979). *The education of Black citizens in Halifax County: 1866–1969.* Springfield, VA: Banister Press.

Elam, S. M., & Rose, L. C. (1995). The 27th annual Phi Delta Kappan/Gallup poll of the public's attitudes toward the public schools. *Phi Delta Kappan, 77,* 41–56.

Ellison, R. (1986). *Going to the territory.* New York: Random House.

Erikson, E. H., & Newton, H. (1973). *In search of common ground: Conversations with Erik H. Erikson and Huey P. Newton.* New York: Norton.

Erskine, N. (1994). *King among the theologians.* Cleveland, OH: Pilgrim Press.

Eugene, T. M. (1989). Sometimes I feel like a motherless child: The call and response for a liberational ethic of care by Black feminists. In M. M. Brabeck (Ed.), *Who cares? Theory, research, and educational implications of the ethic of care* (pp. 45–62). New York: Praeger.

Fanon, F. (1967). *Black skin, White masks.* New York: Grove Press.

Finnan, C., St. John, E. P., Slovacek, S. P., & McCarthy, J. (Eds.) (1996). *Accelerated schools in action.* Thousand Oaks, CA: Corwin.

Fordham, S. (1996). *Blacked out: Dilemmas of race, identity, and success at Capital High.* Chicago: University of Chicago Press.

Forst, M. L., & Blomquist, M. E. (1991). Cracking down on juveniles: The changing ideology of youth corrections. *Notre Dame Journal of Law, Ethics, and Public Policy, 5,* 323–375.

Fossey, R. (1998). Desegregation is not enough: Facing the truth about urban schools. In R. Fossey (Ed.), *Race, the courts, and equal education* (pp. 5–20). New York: AMS Press.

Foster, M. (1990). The politics of race: Through the eyes of African American teachers. *Journal of Education, 172,* 123–141.

Foster, M. (1991). Just got to find a way: Case studies of the lives and practice of exemplary Black high school teachers. In M. Foster (Ed.), *Qualitative investigations into schools and schooling* (pp. 273–309). New York: Aims Press.

Foster, M. (1997). *Black teachers on teaching.* New York: New Press.

Franklin, R. (1990). *Liberating visions: Human fulfillment and social justice in African American thought.* Minneapolis, MN: Fortress Press.

Fry Brown, T. (2000). *God don't like ugly: African American women handing on spiritual values.* Nashville, TN: Abingdon.

Furlong, M., Chung, A., Bates, M., & Morrison, R. (1995). Who are the victims of school violence? *Educational Treatment of Children, 18,* 1–17.

Garbarino, J., Kostelny, K., & Dubrow, N. (1991). What children can tell us about living in danger. *American Psychologist, 46,* 376–383.

Garrod, A., Smulyan, L., Powers, S., & Kilkenny, R. (2002). *Adolescent portraits: Identity, relationships, and challenges.* Boston: Allyn & Bacon.

Garrod, A., Ward, J. V., Robinson, T., & Kilkenny, R. (1999). *Souls looking back: Life stories of growing up black.* New York: Routledge.

Gegax, T., Adler, J., & Pedersen, D. (1998, April 6). The boys behind the ambush. *Newsweek, 131,* 21–24.

Gilligan, C. (1982). *In a different voice: Psychological theory and women's development.* Cambridge, MA: Harvard University Press.

Gilligan, C. (1986a). Exit-voice dilemmas in adolescent development. In A. Foxley, M. McPherson, & G. O'Donnell (Eds.), *Development, democracy, and the art of trespassing* (pp. 283–300). Notre Dame, IN: University of Notre Dame Press.

Gilligan, C. (1986b). Reply (to critics: Kerber, Greeno, Maccoby, Luria, and Stack). *Signs, 11,* 324–333.

Gilligan, C. (1988). The origins of morality in early childhood relationships. In C. Gilligan, J. V. Ward, & J. M. Taylor (Eds.), *Mapping the moral domain* (pp. 111–138). Cambridge, MA: Harvard University Press.

Gilligan, C. (1998). Remembering Larry. *Journal of Moral Education, 27,* 125–140.

Gilligan, C., Lyons, N., & Hanmer, T. J. (1990). *Making connections: The relational worlds of adolescent girls at Emma Willard School.* Cambridge, MA: Harvard University Press.

Gilligan, C., Ward, J. V., Taylor, J. M., & Bardige, B. (Eds.). (1988). *Mapping the moral domain: A contribution of women's thinking to psychological theory and education.* Cambridge, MA: Harvard University Press.

Gilligan, C., & Wiggins, G. (1987). The origins of morality in early childhood relationships. In J. Kagan & S. Lamb (Eds.), *The emergence of morality in young children* (pp. 277–305). Chicago, IL: University of Chicago Press.

Giovanni, N. (1980). Nikki Rosa. In T. Cade (Ed.), *The Black woman* (p. 16). New York: New American Library.

Gorsuch, R. L. (1988). Psychology of religion. *Annual Review of Psychology, 39,* 201–221.

Grant, J. (1998). *Ella Baker: Freedom bound.* New York: John Wiley & Sons.

Gray, L. M. (1993). *Dear Willie Rudd* (P. M. Fiore, Illus.). New York: Simon & Schuster Books for Young Readers.

Green, A. (2002). Review of the book *The skin we're in* by J. Ward. *Journal of Moral Education, 31*(4), 477–479.

Gwaltney, J. (1980). *Drylongso: A self-portrait of Black America.* New York: Random House.

Hansen, D. (2002). The moral environment in an inner-city boys' high school. *Teaching & Teacher Education, 18*(2), 183–204.

Haraway, D. J. (1991). *Simians, cyborgs, and women: The reinvention of nature.* New York: Routledge.

Harding, S. (1987). *Feminism and methodology: Social science issues.* Bloomington: Indiana University Press.

Harding, S. (1998). *Is science multicultural? Postcolonialisms, feminisms, and epistemologies.* Bloomington: Indiana University Press.

Harding, V. (1981). *There is a river: The Black struggle for freedom in America.* San Diego, CA: Harcourt Brace Jovanovich.

Harding, V. (1990). *Hope and history: Why we must share the story of the movement.* Maryknoll, NY: Orbis Books.

Hart, D., Atkins, R., & Ford, D. (1998). Urban America as a context for the development of moral identity in adolescence. *Journal of Social Issues, 54,* 513–530.

Haskins, J. (1986). The triumph of the spirit in nonfiction for Black children. In F. Butler & R. Robert (Eds.), *Triumphs of the spirit in children's literature* (pp. 88–96). Hamden, CT: Library Professional Publications.

Hays, K. (1998, April 26). Boy held in teacher's killing. *The Detroit News and Free Press,* p. 5.

Hecht, M., Collier, M., & Ribeau, S. (1993). *African American communication: Ethnic identity and cultural interpretation.* Newbury Park, CA: Sage.

Heft, J. (1995). Can character be taught? *Journal for a Just and Caring Education, 4,* 389–402.

Hekman, S. J. (1995). *Moral voices, moral selves: Carol Gilligan and feminist moral theory.* University Park: Pennsylvania State University Press.

Henry, A. (1995). Introduction revisited: Better a maroon than a mammy. In J. Gaskell & J. Willinsky (Eds.), *Gender in/forms curriculum* (pp. 15–19). New York: Teachers College Press.

Herskovits, M. J. (1966). The New World Negro: Selected papers in Afroamerican studies. Bloomington: Indiana University Press.

Higgins, A. (1995). Educating for justice and community: Lawrence Kohlberg's vision of moral education. In W. Kurtines & J. Gewirtz (Eds.), *Moral development* (pp. 109–133). Boston: Allyn & Bacon.

Hollingshead, A. (1975). *Four factor index of social status.* Working paper, Department of Sociology, Yale University, New Haven, Connecticut.

hooks, b. (1984). *Feminist theory: From margin to center.* Boston: South End Press.

hooks, b. (1990). *Yearning: Race, gender, and cultural politics.* Boston: South End Press.

hooks, b. (1994). *Teaching to transgress: Education as the practice of freedom.* New York: Routledge.

hooks, b. (2000). *All about love: New visions.* New York: William Morrow.

Hughes, L. (1969). *Black misery.* New York: Oxford University Press.

Hume, D. (1875). *The philosophical works of David Hume* (4 vols.). London: Longmans, Green.

Hundley, M. G. (1965). *The Dunbar story (1870–1955)*. New York: Vantage Press.

Hurtado, A. (1996). Strategic suspensions: Feminists of color theorize the production of knowledge. In N. R. Goldberger (Ed.), *Knowledge, difference, and power* (pp. 372–392). New York: Basic Books.

Hutchinson, G. (1939, April). Jim Crow challenged in southern universities. *The Crisis, 105.*

Irvine, J. J. (1990). *Black students and school failure: Policies, practices, and prescriptions.* New York: Greenwood Press.

Irvine, J. J. (2000). Afrocentric education: Critical questions for further consideration. In D. S. Pollard and C. S. Ajirotutu (Eds.), *African-centered schooling in theory and practice* (pp. 199–210). Westport, CN: Bergin & Garvey.

Irvine, J. J. (2002). *In search of wholeness: African American teachers and their culturally specific classroom practices.* New York: Palgrave.

Irvine, R. W., & Irvine, J. J. (1983). The impact of the desegregation process on the education of Black students. *Journal of Negro Education, 52,* 410–421.

Jaffee, S. & Hyde, J. (2000). Gender differences in moral orientation: A meta-analysis. *Psychological Bulletin, 126*(5), 703–726.

James, S. M. (1993). Mothering: A possible Black feminist link to social transformation? In S. M. James & A. P. A. Busia (Eds.), *Theorizing Black feminisms* (pp. 44–54). London: Routledge.

Jefferies, R. (1994). The trickster figure in African American teaching: Pre- and post-desegregation. *The Urban Review, 26,* 289–304.

Jervis, K. (1996). "How come there are no brothers on that list?" Hearing the hard questions all children ask. *Harvard Educational Review, 66,* 546–576.

Johnson, J. W. (1933). *Along this way: The autobiography of James Weldon Johnson.* New York: Viking.

Johnston, B. (1997). *Morality, culture, power: Developing a language of morality for teaching across cultures.* Paper presented at the annual conference of the Association for Moral Education, Atlanta, GA.

Jones, F. (1981). *A traditional model of educational excellence: Dunbar High School of Little Rock, Arkansas.* Washington, DC: Howard University Press.

Jordan, J. (1985). *On call.* Boston: South End Press.

Kailin, J. (1999). How White teachers perceive the problem of racism in their schools: A case study in "liberal" Lakeview. *Teachers College Record, 100,* 724–750.

Kallen, H. M. (1956). Cultural pluralism and the American idea. Philadelphia: University of Pennsylvania Press.

Kant, I. (1797). *The metaphysics of morals, Part I: Metaphysical elements of justice.* Indianapolis, IN: Hackett.

Kelley, R. (1997). *Yo' mamma's disfunktional! Fighting culture wars in urban America.* Boston: Beacon Press.

Kelly, J. (1998). *Under the gaze: Learning to be Black in White society.* Halifax, Nova Scotia: Fernwood.

Kincheloe, J. L. (1993). The politics of race, history, and curriculum. In L. A. Castenell Jr. & W. F. Pinar (Eds.), *Understanding curriculum as racial text* (pp. 249–262). Albany: State University of New York Press.

King, J. E., & Mitchell, C. A. (1995). *Black mothers to sons: Juxtaposing African American literature with social practice* (Rev. ed.). New York: Peter Lang.

King, M. L., Jr. (1963a, August 28). I have a dream. [Speech at Lincoln Memorial, Washington, DC] (Reprinted in *Ebony*, January, 1986, pp. 40–42.)

King, M. L., Jr. (1963b, April 16). Letter from Birmingham Jail. In *Why we can't wait* (pp. 76–95). New York: Signet.

King, M. L., Jr. (1963c). *Strength to love.* New York: Harper & Row.

King, M. L., Jr. (1967a, May). Declaration of independence from the war in Vietnam: Condensed version of an address delivered at the Riverside Church in New York on April 4, 1967. *Ramparts*, pp. 33–37.

King, M. L., Jr. (1967b, Spring). A time to break silence: Full version of an address delivered at the Riverside Church in New York on April 4, 1967. *Freedomways*, pp. 103–117.

King, M. L., Jr. (1967c). *Where do we go from here: Chaos or community?* New York: Harper & Row.

King, M. L., Jr. (1986). *Testament of hope: The essential writings and speeches of Martin Luther King, Jr.* (M. Washington, Ed.). San Francisco: Harper Collins.

Kirby, B. (1998, November). *Hanging by the backs of our knees: Education and racism.* Paper presented at the annual meeting of the American Educational Studies Association, Philadelphia.

Kluger, R. (1977). *Simple justice.* New York: Random House.

Kohl, H. (1995). The story of Rosa Parks and the Montgomery Bus Boycott revisited. In *Should we burn Babar? Essays on children's literature and the power of stories* (pp. 30–56). New York: New Press.

Kohlberg, L. (1968a, Spring). Education for justice. Lecture delivered at the Harvard Graduate School of Education. Reprinted in N. F. Sizer & T. R. Sizer (Eds.) (1970), *Moral education* (pp. 57–84). Cambridge, MA: Harvard University Press.

Kohlberg, L. (1968b). Letter to Edward Levi, President–Elect of the University of Chicago. Papers of Lawrence Kohlberg: Correspondence (box 5). Harvard University Archives, Cambridge, MA.

Kohlberg, L. (1970). Course description and outline for social sciences 154, Moral and Political Choice, included in Toward a Proposal for a Textbook for the Course. Papers of Lawrence Kohlberg: Teaching materials (box 3). Harvard University Archives, Cambridge, MA.

Kohlberg, L. (1975). Course description and outline for social sciences 154,

Moral and Political Choice, included in Proposal for a General Education Seminar. Papers of Lawrence Kohlberg: Teaching materials (box 2). Harvard University Archives, Cambridge, MA.

Kohlberg, L. (1981). *The philosophy of moral development: Moral stages and the idea of justice.* (*Essays on moral development*, Vol. 1). San Francisco: Harper & Row.

Kohlberg, L. (1984). *The psychology of moral development: The nature and validity of moral stages.* (*Essays on moral development*, Vol. 2). San Francisco: Harper & Row.

Kohlberg, L., & Davidson, F. (1975, March). The cognitive-developmental approach to inter-ethnic attitudes: Abstract of paper for A.P.L. Papers of Lawrence Kohlberg: Manuscripts and Related Papers (box 16). Harvard University Archives, Cambridge, MA.

Kohlberg, L., & Mayer, R. (1972). Development as the aim of education. *Harvard Educational Review, 42,* 449–496.

Kohlberg, L., & Power, F. C. (1981). Moral development, religious thinking, and the question of a seventh stage. In L. Kohlberg, *Essays on moral development. Volume 1. The philosophy of moral development* (pp. 311–372). New York: Harper & Row.

Kuhmerker, L. (1991). *The Kohlberg legacy for the helping professions.* Birmingham, AL: REP Books.

Kuhn, D., & Udell, W. (2001). The path to wisdom. *Educational Psychologist, 36*(4), 261–264.

Kuhn, T. S. (1962). *The structure of scientific revolutions.* Chicago: University of Chicago Press.

Kuther, T., & Wallace, S. (2003). Community violence and sociomoral development: An African American cultural perspective. *American Journal of Orthopsychiatry, 73*(2), 177–189.

Ladd, G., & Cairns, E. (1996). Children: Ethnic and political violence. *Child Development, 67,* 14–18.

Ladner, J. (Ed.) (1973). *The death of White sociology: Essays on race and culture.* Baltimore: Black Classic Press.

Ladson-Billings, G. (1994). *The dream keepers: Successful teachers of African American children.* San Francisco: Jossey-Bass.

Ladson-Billings, G. (2000). Fighting for our lives: Preparing teachers to teach African American students. *Journal of Teacher Education, 51*(3), 206–214.

Lamme, L. (1996). Digging deeply: Morals and ethics in children's literature. *Journal for a Just and Caring Education, 2,* 411–419.

Littlefield, V. (1999). *Annie Holland and the struggle to educate North Carolina's neglected.* Unpublished paper.

Locke, A. L. (1935). Values and imperatives. In S. Hook and H. M. Kallen (Eds.), *American philosophy today and tomorrow* (pp. 313–333). New York: Furman.

Lorde, A. (1984). *Sister outsider: Essays and speeches.* Freedom, CA: Crossing Press.

Mama, A. (1995). *Beyond the masks: Race, gender, and subjectivity.* London: Routledge.

Martin, J. R. (1992). *The school home: Rethinking schools for changing families.* Cambridge, MA: Harvard University Press.

Mayeroff, M. (1971). *On caring.* New York: Harper & Row.

McAllister, G. (1997). *A home away from home: Care and justice in an African American after-school program.* Paper presented at the 1997 annual conference of the Association for Moral Education, Atlanta, GA.

McAllister, G., & Irvine, J. S. (2000). Cross cultural competency and multicultural teacher education. *Review of Educational Research, 70*(1), 3–24.

McCullough-Garrett, A. (1993). Reclaiming the African American vision for teaching: Toward an educational conversation. *Journal of Negro Education, 62,* 433–440.

McDonough, P. M., Antonio, A. L., & Trent, J. W. (1997). Black students, Black colleges: An African-American college choice model. *Journal for a Just and Caring Education, 3,* 9–36.

Merton, R. (1973). *The sociology of science.* Chicago: University of Chicago Press.

Miron, L. F., St. John, E. P., & Davidson, B. (1998). Implementing school restructuring in the inner city. *The Urban Review, 30*(2), 137–166.

Monroe, C. (2003). Review of the book *Peer harassment in school. Journal of Moral Education, 31*(3), 209–211.

Morris, B. (1997). Bernadine B. Morris [autobiography]. In M. Foster & L. Delpit (Eds.), *Black teachers on teaching* (pp. 53–61). New York: New Press.

Morris, V. G., & Morris, C. L. (2000). *Creating caring and nurturing educational environments for African American children.* Denver: Bergin & Garvey.

Morrison, G. M., Furlong, M. J., & Morrison, R. L. (1997). The safe school: Moving beyond crime prevention to school empowerment. In A. P. Goldstein & J. C. Conoley (Eds.), *School violence intervention.* New York: Guilford Press.

Morrison, T. (1992). *Playing in the dark: Whiteness and the literary imagination.* New York: Vintage Books.

Murray, P. (1987). *Song in a weary throat: An American Pilgrimage.* New York: Harper & Row.

Nettles, M. T., & Perna, L. (1997). *The African American education data book: Vol. 2. Preschool through high school education.* Fairfax, VA: Frederick D. Patterson Research Institute of the United Negro College Fund.

Nettles, M. T., & Perna, L. (2000). Salary, promotion, and tenure of minority ands women faculty in U.S. colleges and universities. *Education Statistics Quarterly, 2*(2), 94–96.

Noblit, G. (1993). Power and caring. *American Educational Research Journal, 30,* 23–38.

Noblit, G., & Dempsey, V. (1996). *The social construction of virtue: The moral life of schools.* Albany: State University of New York Press.

Noddings, N. (1984). *Caring: A feminine approach to ethics and moral education.* Berkeley: University of California Press.

Noddings, N. (1988). An ethic of caring and its implications for instructional arrangements. *American Journal of Education, 96,* 215–230.

Noddings, N. (1989). *Women and evil.* Berkeley: University of California Press.

Noddings, N. (1992). *The challenge to care in schools: An alternative approach to education.* New York: Teachers College Press.

Noddings, N. (1993). *Educating for intelligent belief and unbelief.* New York: Teachers College Press.

Noddings, N. (1995, May). Teaching themes of care. *Phi Delta Kappan,* 675–679.

Noddings, N. (1999). Care, justice, and equity. In M. Katz, N. Noddings, & K. Strike (Eds.), *Justice and caring* (pp. 7–20). New York: Teachers College Press.

Noddings, N. (2002). *Starting at home: Caring and social policy.* Berkeley, CA: University of California Press.

Noguera, P. A. (1995). Preventing and producing violence: A critical analysis of responses to school violence. *Harvard Educational Review, 51,* 189–212.

Nussbaum, M. C. (2000). *Sex and social justice.* New York: Oxford University Press.

Obidah, J. E. (2000). Mediating boundaries of race, class, and professional authority as a critical multiculturalist. *Teachers College Record, 102*(6), 1035–1060.

Obidah, J., & Teel, K. (2001). *Because of the kids: Confronting racial and cultural differences.* New York: Teachers College Press.

Office of Management and Budget. (1997). *Recommendations from the Interagency Committee for the review of the racial and ethnic standards to the Office of Management and Budget concerning changes to the standards for the classification of federal data on race and ethnicity.* Washington, DC: Office of Management and Budget.

Olinga (Jones), A. (1981). *The oppression syndrome of Africans colonized in the United States.* Unpublished doctoral dissertation, University of Massachusetts, Amherst, MA.

Orfield, G., Frankenberg, E., & Lee, C. (2002) The resurgence of school segregation. *Educational Leadership, 60*(4), 16–20.

Pajares, F., & Graham, L. (1997). *Teachers' and students' beliefs about truth and caring in the teaching conversation.* Paper presented at the Association for Moral Education Annual Conference, Emory University, Atlanta.

Parham, T., & Williams, P. (1993). The relationship of demographic and background factors to racial identity attitudes. *Journal of Black Psychology, 19,* 7–24.

Paris, P. J. (1995). *The spirituality of African peoples.* Minneapolis: Fortress Press.

Parke, R. D. (2000). Beyond White and middle class: Cultural variations in families-assessments, processes, and policies. *Journal of Family Psychology, 14*(3), 331–333.

Peart, N., & Campbell, F. (1999) At-risk students' perceptions of teacher effectiveness. *Journal for a Just and Caring Education, 5,* 269–284.

Power, F. C., Higgins, A., & Kohlberg, L. (1989). *Lawrence Kohlberg's approach to moral education.* New York: Columbia University Press.

Prothrow-Stith, D. (1991). *Deadly consequences.* New York: HarperCollins.

Puka, B. (1994a). *Moral development: Vol. 5. New research in moral development.* Hamden, CT: Garland.

Puka, B. (1994b). *Moral development: Vol. 6. Caring voices and women's moral frames.* Hamden, CT: Garland.

Ramirez, M., & Castaneda, A. (1974). *Cultural democracy.* New York: Longman.

Raphael, D. (2001). *Concepts of justice.* New York: Oxford University Press.

Rashid, H. (1984, January). Promoting biculturalism in young African-American children. *Young Children, 39,* 13–23.

Rawls, J. (1971). *A theory of justice.* Cambridge, MA: Harvard University Press.

Razack, S. H. (1998). *Looking White people in the eye: Gender, race, and culture in courtrooms and classrooms.* Toronto: University of Toronto Press.

Reimer, J., Paolitto, D. P., & Hersh, R. H. (1983). *Promoting moral growth: From Piaget to Kohlberg* (2nd ed.). New York: Longman.

Ringgold, F. (1991). *Tar beach.* New York: Crown.

Ringgold, F. (1995). *We flew over the bridge: The memoirs of Faith Ringgold.* Boston: Bulfinch/Little, Brown.

Ringgold, F., Freeman, L., & Roucher, N. (1996). *Talking to Faith Ringgold.* New York: Crown.

Rodgers, F. (1976). *The Black high school and its community.* Lexington, MA: Lexington Books.

Rorty, R. (1999). *Philosophy and social hope.* New York: Penguin.

Rose, L. C., Gallup, A. M., Elam, S. M. (1997). The 29th annual Phi Delta Kappan/Gallup poll of the public's attitudes toward the public schools. *Phi Delta Kappan, 79,* 41–56.

Sadker, M., & Sadker, D. (1997). *Teachers, schools, and society.* (4th ed.) New York: McGraw-Hill.

St. John, E. P., Griffith, A. I., & Allen-Haynes, L. (1997). *Families in schools: A chorus of voices in restructuring.* Portsmouth, NH: Heinemann.

Schneider, A., & Schramm, D. (1986). The Washington state juvenile justice system reform: A review of findings. *Criminal Justice and Policy Review, 211,* 231–232.

Schultz, S. (1973). *The culture factory: Boston public schools, 1789–1860.* New York: Oxford University Press.

Shade, B. J. (1994). Understanding the African American learner. In E. R. Hollins, J. E. King, & W. C. Hayman (Eds.), *Teaching diverse populations* (pp. 175–190). Albany: State University of New York Press.

Siddle Walker, V. (1993a). Caswell County Training School, 1933–69: Relationships between community and school. *Harvard Educational Review, 63,* 161–181.

Siddle Walker, V. (1993b). Interpersonal caring in the "good" segregated schooling of African American children. *Urban Review, 25,* 63–77.

Siddle Walker, V. (1996). *Their highest potential: An African American school community in the segregated South.* Chapel Hill: University of North Carolina Press.

Siddle Walker, V. (1998). Commentary: Focus on diversity. *AACTE Briefs, 19,* 4–5, 8.

Siddle Walker, V. (2000). Valued segregated schools for African American children in the South, 1935–1969: A review of common themes and characteristics. *Review of Educational Research, 70,* 253–285.

Simpson, E. L. (1974). Moral development research: A case study of scientific cultural bias. *Human Development, 17,* 81–106.

Sims, R. (1982). *Shadow and substance: Afro-American experience in contemporary children's fiction.* Urbana, IL: National Council of Teachers of English.

Skoe, E. (1991). A measure of care-based morality and its relation to ego identity. *Merrill-Palmer Quarterly, 37,* 289–304.

Skoe, E. (1993). *The ethic of care interview manual.* Tromso, Norway: University of Tromso.

Slack, J. B., & St. John, E. P. (1999, April). *A practical model for measuring the effect of school reform on the reading achievement of non-transient learners.* Presented at the annual meeting of the American Educational Research Association, Montreal, Canada.

Slaughter-Defoe, D. (1991). Parental educational choice: Some African American dilemmas. *Journal of Negro Education, 60*(3), 354–360.

Slaughter-Defoe, D. T., & Carlson, K. G. (1997). Young African American and Latino children in high poverty urban schools: How they perceive school climate. *Journal of Negro Education, 65,* 50–70.

Smith, L. (1991). *The mystic as prophet.* Richmond, IN: Friends United Press.

Smith, T. (1994). King and the black religious quest to cure racism. In M I. Wallace & T. H. Smith (Eds.), *Curing violence* (230–237). Sonoma, CA: Polebridge Press.

Snarey, J. (1985). Cross-cultural universality of social-moral development: A critical review of Kohlbergian research, *Psychological Bulletin, 97,* 202–232.

Snarey, J. (1992). Moral education. *Encyclopedia of educational research* (Vol. 3, pp. 856–860). New York: Macmillan.

Snarey, J. (1995). In a communitarian voice: The sociological expansion of Kohlbergian theory, research, and practice. In W. Kurtines & J. Gewirtz (Eds.), *Moral development* (pp. 109–133). Boston: Allyn & Bacon.

Sowell, T. (1974). Black excellence: The case of Dunbar High School. *Public Interest, 35*, 1–21.

Sowell, T. (1976). Patterns of Black excellence. *Public Interest, 43*, 26–58.

Spencer, M. B. (1988). Self-concept development. In D. T. Slaughter (Ed.), *Black children and poverty: A developmental perspective* (pp. 59–72). San Francisco: Jossey-Bass.

Spencer, M. B. (1999). Social and cultural influences on school adjustment: The application of an identity-focused cultural ecological perspective. *Educational Psychologist, 34*(1), 43–57.

Spencer, M. B., Fegley, S., & Harpalani, V. (2003). A theoretical and empirical examination of identity as coping: Linking coping resources to self processes of African American youth. *Applied Developmental Science, 7*(3), 181–188.

Spencer, M. B., Noll, E., Stoltzfus, J., & Harpalani, V. (2001). Identity and school adjustment: Revisiting the "acting White" assumption. *Educational Psychologist, 36*(1), 21–30.

Strike, K., Haller, E., & Soltis, J. (1998). *The ethics of school administration.* New York: Teachers College Press.

Taylor, C. (1985). *Human agency and language: Philosophical papers.* New York: Cambridge University Press.

Taylor, J. M., Gilligan, C., & Sullivan, A. M. (1995). *Between voice and silence: Women and girls, race and relationship.* Cambridge, MA: Harvard University Press.

Teddlie, C. (1998). Four literatures associated with the study of equal education and desegregation in the United States. In R. Fossey (Ed.), *Race, the courts, and equal education* (pp. 237–258). New York: AMS Press.

Thoma, S. (1986). Estimating gender differences in the comprehension and preference of moral issues. *Developmental Review, 6*(2), 165–180.

Thompson, A. (1999). Colortalk: Whiteness and off white. *Educational Studies, 30*, 141–160.

Thompson, A. (2001). Harriet Tubman in pictures: Cultural consciousness and the art of picture books. *The Lion and the Unicorn, 25*, 81–114.

Thurman, H. (1971). *The search for common ground.* Richmond, IN: Friends United Press.

Tice, K. W. (1998). Mending Rosa's "working ways": A case study of an African American mother and breadwinner. In M. Ladd-Taylor & L. Umansky (Eds.), *"Bad" mothers* (pp. 31–40). New York: New York University Press.

Tilford-Weathers, T. C. (1996). *A history of Louisville Central High School, 1882–1982.* (2nd ed.) Louisville, KY: Central High School Alumni Association (originally self-published in 1982).

Tompkins, R. (2003). Review of two books, *Why is it so hard to get good schools?* by L. Cuban, and *Powerful reforms with shallow roots: Improving America's urban schools,* by L. Cuban and M. Usdan. *Journal of Moral Education, 32*(3), 311–314.

Ture, K., & Hamilton, C. (1992). *Black power: The politics of liberation.* New York: Vintage Books.

Turiel, E. (1994). Morality, authoritarianism, and personal agency in cultural contexts. In R. Sternberg & P. Ruzgis (Eds.), *Personality and intelligence* (pp. 271–299). Cambridge, UK: Cambridge University Press.

Tyree, C., Vance, M., & McJunkin, M. (1997). Teaching values to promote a more caring world. *Journal for a Just and Caring Education, 3,* 215–226.

Valentine, C. (1971). Deficit, difference, bicultural models of Afro-American behavior. *Harvard Educational Review, 41,* 137–157.

Vozzola, E. C. (1997). *In a different method: Examining a real world affirmative action dilemma.* Paper presented at the annual conference of the Association for Moral Education, Atlanta, Georgia.

Walker, A. (1983). *In search of our mothers' gardens: Womanist prose.* New York: Harcourt, Brace, Jovanovich.

Walker, A. (1992). *The color purple.* New York: Harcourt Brace Jovanovich. (Originally published 1982)

Walker, L. (1995). Sexism in Kohlberg's moral psychology? In W. Kurtines & J. Gewritz (Eds.), *Moral development* (pp. 83–107). Boston, MA: Allyn & Bacon.

Ward, J. V. (1988). Urban adolescents' conceptions of violence. In C. Gilligan, J. Ward, & J. Taylor (Eds.), *Mapping the moral domain* (pp. 175–200). Cambridge, MA: Harvard University Press.

Ward, J. V. (1990). Racial identity formation and transformation. In C. Gilligan, N. Lyons, & T. J. Hamner (Eds.), *Making connections* (pp. 215–232). Cambridge, MA: Harvard University Press.

Ward, J. V. (1991). "Eyes in the back of your head": Moral themes in African American narratives of racial conflict. *Journal of Moral Education, 20*(3), 267–281.

Ward, J. V. (1995). Cultivating a morality of care in African American adolescents: A culture-based model of violence prevention. *Harvard Educational Review, 65,* 175–188.

Ward, J. V. (2000). *The skin we're in: Teaching our children to be socially smart, emotionally strong, spiritually connected.* New York: Free Press.

Wark, G., & Krebs, D. (1996). Gender and dilemma differences in real-life moral judgment. *Developmental Psychology, 332*(2), 220–230.

Warner, B. S., & Weist, M. D. (1996). Urban youth as witness to violence: Beginning assessment and treatment efforts. *Journal of Youth and Adolescence, 25*(3), 361–377.

Washington, B. T. (1901). *Up from slavery: An autobiography.* Garden City, NY: Doubleday.

Washington, B. T. (1903). *Character building.* New York: Doubleday, Page.

Williams, D., & Williams-Morris, R. (2002). Racism and mental health: The African American experience. *Ethnicity & Health, 5*(3–4), 243–268.

Wilson, A. N. (1978). *The developmental psychology of the Black child.* New York: Africana Research.

Witkin, G., Tharp, M., Schrof, J., Toch, T., & Scattarella, C. (1998, June 1). Again in Springfield, a familiar school scene: Bloody kids, grieving parents, a teen accused of murder. *U.S. News & World Report, 124,* 16–21.

Woldemikael, T. (1987). Assertion versus accommodation: A comparative approach to intergroup relations. *American Behavioral Scientist, 30*(4), 411–428.

Woodson, C. G. (1972). *The mis-education of the Negro.* Washington, DC: Associated. (Original work published 1933)

X, Malcolm (1970). *By any means necessary: Speeches, interviews, and a letter.* New York: Pathfinder Press.

Yancy, G. (2000). Feminism and the subtext of Whiteness: Black women's experiences as a site of identity formation and contestation of Whiteness. *Western Journal of Black Studies, 24*(3), 156–166.

About the Editors and Contributors

Vanessa Siddle Walker received her Ed.D. from Harvard University and is currently Winship Distinguished Research Professor in the Division of Educational Studies at Emory University (Atlanta). Her research interests focus on the historical and cultural influences on the teaching and learning of African American students. Dr. Siddle Walker has received the Raymond Cattell Early Career Award from the American Educational Research Association and the Grawemeyer Award in Education.

John R. Snarey received his Ed.D. from Harvard University and is professor of human development and ethics in the Candler School of Theology and the Department of Psychology at Emory University (Atlanta). His research interests include the longitudinal, cross-cultural, and neuroscience study of moral development. Dr. Snarey, President-elect of the Association for Moral Education, has received the Outstanding Human Development Research Award from the American Educational Research Association.

Charles D. Blakeney received his Ed.D. from Harvard University and is director emeritus of the Institute for Clinical Developmental Psychology, Los Angeles. Dr. Blakeney is currently a visiting professor in the Department of Education, University of Fribourg, Switzerland. His ongoing research interests are moral formation and the developmental sequelae of childhood trauma among African American men. Dr. Blakeney has served as principal consultant to the California State Assembly and the Massachusetts State House.

Ronnie Frankel Blakeney received her Ed.D. from Harvard University and is director of the Institute for Clinical Developmental Psychology in Los Angeles. Dr. Blakeney is currently a visiting professor in the Department of Education, University of Fribourg, Switzerland. Her ongoing research interests include moral formation and cross-cultural communication. Dr. Blakeney served as a consultant to the White House Office of Domestic Policy and many other public and private organizations.

Joseph P. Cadray received his Ph.D. from the University of New Orleans and is currently assistant professor of education in the Division of Educational Studies at Emory University. He is interested in reflective practice and cultural responsiveness in teacher education, urban education, multicultural education, and higher education.

Garrett Albert Duncan received his Ph.D. from the Claremont Graduate School and is associate professor of education and of African and Afro-American studies at Washington University in Saint Louis. His research interests center on race and adolescent development. A former public school teacher, Dr. Duncan was named Teacher of the Year by the students of Pomona High School (CA); he is the recipient of an American Educational Research Grant from the U.S. Department of Education.

Andrea D. Green is a doctoral candidate in the Graduate Division of Religion and an adjunct instructor in the Candler School of Theology at Emory University. Her research focuses on using the tools of developmental psychology and practical theology to explore the dynamics of moral formation among African American women.

Marquita Jackson-Minot received her Ph.D. in urban studies at Emory University and is currently assistant professor of education at Agnes Scott College. Her research interests focus on urban education and on school climate and care as they influence student achievement.

Carla R. Monroe is a doctoral candidate in the Division of Educational Studies at Emory University. Her research interests include educational methods for promoting care and justice in urban schools and for promoting second language acquisition. Carla Monroe is currently a Spencer Foundation Fellow.

Jennifer E. Obidah received her Ph.D. from the University of California at Berkeley and is associate professor of educational studies at the University of California at Los Angeles. Her area of interest is the social and cultural context of urban schooling, focusing on issues of violence, multicultural education, and teacher preparation. Dr. Obidah is the recipient of a research fellowship from the National Institute of Mental Health.

Edward P. St. John received his Ed.D. from Harvard University and is currently professor of educational leadership and policy studies and Director of the Education Policy Center at Indiana University. His research has focused on policy issues in higher education, educational improvement in diverse settings, and the impact of financial aid on educational opportunity. Dr. St. John received the Robert P. Huff Golden Quill Award from the National Association of Financial Aid Administrators.

Audrey Thompson received her Ph.D. from the University of Illinois at Urbana-Champaign and is currently professor of philosophy of education and gender studies in the Department of Education, Culture, and Society at the University of Utah. Her research addresses feminist ethics, antiracist pedagogy, African American epistemology, and moral and aesthetic education. Dr. Thompson has received the College of Education Faculty Research Award at the University of Utah.

Renarta H. Tompkins is a doctoral candidate in the Division of Educational Studies at Emory University. Her research focuses upon literacy development among at-risk students during the elementary school years.

Brian Williams received his Ph.D. in educational studies at Emory University and is currently a visiting professor at Abbiyi Addi College of Teacher Education in Tigray, Ethiopia. His research interests include justice ethics and improving the representation of people of color in science, mathematics, and engineering. He is the recipient of a Ford Foundation Fellowship.

Index